Eat London

Written by Joe Warwick

HG2 EAT LONDON

Managing director – Tremayne Carew Pole
Marketing director – Sara Townsend
Series editor – Catherine Blake
Design – Nick Randall
Maps – Amber Sheers and Nick Randall
Repro – Dorchester Typesetting
Printers – Printed in China by Leo
Publisher – Filmer Ltd

Photography by Ben Illis

Additional research by Jo Monk, Louise McGough

Email – info@hg2.com
Website – www.hg2.com

First published in the United Kingdom in November 2008
by
Filmer Ltd
17 Shawfield St
London SW3 4BA

ISBN – 978-1-905428-27-4

There are those that think compiling lists is cultural fascism. Unfortunately, I seem to have spent much of my career so far doing it – so call me a cultural fascist. Or maybe it's just that I'm quite easily led.

I've done lists of the best, the greatest and even on one occasion – when I was really down on my luck – the sexiest. I've done chef lists, people lists, food feud lists, lists of fake foods, cider lists, lists of excuses for being late and of course, lists of restaurants. In compiling these lists I've often declared them arbitrary and pointless.

Not so the list of restaurants in this book or the many lists over the next couple of pages – they're all good lists – really they are. All of which naturally make an informative and entertaining read.

The 150 restaurants featured here come through the recommendations of a sizeable number of London's restaurant insiders; critics, chefs, dairy godfathers, restaurateurs, PRs, headhunters, managers, executives, editors, and food and wine writers. I'd like to thank them all for their help and their time. They're listed in full on page 5 onwards.

They're all full-time London residents, with the exception of a few that flit about, the jet-setter chefs and restaurateurs, but who still spend a lot of time here. That's important because I wanted their opinions not just as restaurant industry types but also as Londoners.

They were all asked to recommend – NOT THE BEST – but what they thought were the best places to go and eat for specific situations, from when funds were tight, to when someone else is picking up the tab, from having breakfast to eating late at night, from eating in a hurry to relaxing on a Sunday. There's a full list of all the questions they were asked on page 8.

One hundred and fifty isn't a lot of restaurants, unless of course you have to write 150 reviews, and there are easily enough interesting restaurants out there to fill much bigger books than this, which they do. But although there's nothing definitive about this little book I'd like to think that doesn't stop it being useful, with advice for where to eat, when to eat there and what to order.

As a guide the little pink price in the bottom right hand corner of each review is the approximate cost of two courses with half a bottle of wine.

In the process of putting all this together I discovered places I'd never heard of, others I'd heard of but never been to. I was also reminded of restaurants, old favourites where I haven't been for too long, as I seem to spend much of my time running around after the latest new opening.

Good restaurants are like faithful friends, I've since decided, and you should never neglect them just because someone younger and flashier suddenly comes into your life. Accordingly the selection of restaurants included here is a good mix of pretty young things and more seasoned performers.

Aside from hopefully keeping myself in clean underpants for the next year with the proceeds from this book, I also hope it will inspire anyone that picks it up to eat out a little bit more around the city in general. London has acres of fantastic restaurants that deserve your attention. I hope the small, well-chosen selection here whets your appetite to explore further.

Go out, eat, and enjoy yourself.

Joe Warwick

Contributors

Adam Byatt chef proprietor, Trinity Restaurant
Aiden Byrne head chef, The Grill at The Dorchester
Alan Yau restaurateur, Hakkasan, Yauatcha, Cha Cha Moon, Sake No Hana
Angela Hartnett chef proprietor, Murano
Anna Hansen chef proprietor, The Modern Pantry
Anna Longmore food & drink writer, Square Meal magazine
Anouska Menzies director, Bacchus PR
Anthony Demetre chef proprietor, Arbutus and Wild Honey
Antonin Bonnet head chef, The Greenhouse
Ben McCormack editor, Square Meal magazine
Bill Knott food & drink writer, roaming editor Yes Chef!
Caroline Davy director, JRPR
Caroline Stacey food writer & freelance critic for the Independent
Carolyn Cavele director, Food Matters
Charles Campion food writer, editor of The London Restaurant Guide
Chris Barber food consultant
Chris Maillard journalist & editor
Chris Wood managing director, Toptable
Christian Sandefeldt chef proprietor, Deep
Claude Bosi chef proprietor, Hibiscus
Claudio Pulze restaurateur, The Cuisine Collection
Dai Francis restaurant industry supplier
Darren Neilan restaurant manager, One-o-One
David Lancaster journalist & consultant
Dominic Chapman head chef, The Royal Oak Paley Street, Berkshire
Duncan Ackery chief executive, Searcy's
Fay Maschler restaurant critic, Evening Standard
Fergus Henderson chef proprietor, St John/ St John Bread & Wine
Franceso Mazzei chef proprietor, L'Anima
Frederic Serol operations manager, MARC Restaurants
Gary Rhodes chef proprietor, Rhodes W1/Rhodes 24

Giles Coren restaurant critic, The Times
Guillaume Rochette managing director, Eureka Executive Search
Henry Harris chef proprietor, Racine
Heston Blumenthal chef proprietor, The Fat Duck, Berkshire
Hilary Armstrong food & drink journalist, London Lite
Ichiro Kubota head chef, Umu, London W1
Irena Pogarcic director, Kitchen Communications
Jacinta Phelan general manager, Harvey Nichols Restaurants
James Aufenast managing editor, Caterer & Hotelkeeper
Jancis Robinson wine writer, Financial Times
Jason Atherton head chef, Maze
Jay Rayner restaurant critic, The Observer
Jennifer Sharp journalist, editor & restaurant critic
Jeremy Lee head chef, Blueprint Café
Jerome Armit restaurant manager, Crazy Bear
Jo Barnes director, Sauce Communications
John Nugent chief executive, Green & Fortune
John-Christophe Ansanay-Alex chef proprietor, L'Ambassade de l'Ile
Jonas Karlsson executive chef, Harvey Nichols 5th Floor Restaurant
Kate Spicer freelance journalist, Sunday Times
Laurie Fletcher restaurant industry photographer
Marina O'Loughlin restaurant critic, Metro London
Margot Henderson restaurateur and caterer, Rochelle Canteen/Arnold & Henderson
Mark Edwards executive chef, Nobu Europe
Mark Hix chef proprietor, Hix Oyster & Chop House
Maureen Mills owner, Network London PR
Morgan Meunier chef proprietor, Morgan M
Mourad Mazouz restaurateur, Momo, Sketch
Nick Harman editor, London-Eating.co.uk
Nick Jones CEO/founder, Soho House Group
Oliver Peyton restaurateur, Peyton & Byrne/Peyton Restaurants
Pat McDonald chef/consultant, The Ford McDonald consultancy

Pat Williams chef proprietor, The Terrace in the Fields

Pierre Gagnaire consultant chef, Sketch

Pierre Koffman executive chef, Brasserie St Jacques,

Rainer Becker chef proprietor, Zuma/Roka

Raymond de Fazio restaurateur

Richard Corrigan chef proprietor, Bentleys/Lindsay House

Rowley Leigh chef proprietor, Le Café Anglais

Roy Ackerman restaurant consultant

Simon Binder restaurant consultant

Sinead Mallozzi CEO, Sketch

Summer Litchfield restaurant writer, Urban Junkies

Terry Durack restaurant critic, The Independent on Sunday

Tom Aikens chef proprietor, Tom Aikens, Tom's Place, Tom's Kitchen

Tom Ilic chef proprietor, Tom Ilic

Tom Kerridge chef proprietor, The Hand & Flowers, Buckinghamshire

Tom Parker Bowles food writer, The Mail on Sunday

Tom Pemberton chef proprietor, Hereford Road

Tracey MacLeod restaurant critic, The Independent

Trevor Gulliver restaurateur, St John/St John Bread & Wine/Brew Wharf

William Sitwell editor, Waitrose Food Illustrated

Zoe Williams restaurant critic, The Sunday Telegraph

The Questions

Please pick one place in London (which for the basis of this survey does not go beyond Zone 3 on the Tube) that's your first choice for each of the following, giving reasons where possible:

1. Dining solo for the occasional pleasure that is eating alone

2. Lazy Sunday for brunch or lunch, possibly whilst nursing a hangover

3. Breakfast be it early morning sustenance or when it just too long until lunch

4. On-the-hoof from favourite takeaways to anywhere where it's possible to eat and run

5. Frugal feasting bona fide bargains for when funds are tight

6. **Abusing the wine list** liver be damned

7. Clandestine rendezvous when you don't want to run into anyone you know

8. Making an impression whether it's for business or treating someone special

9. Being pampered where the service makes you feel like royalty

10. Open-all-hours nocturnal nibbles

11. Pub grub good beer and something to soak it up

12. When someone else is paying no-expense spared meal anywhere you want

13. One-of-a-kind London experience from the best view of The Thames to that little place you know deep in the East End with the transvestite belly dancers

14. People-watching where – good eating aside – the scene's the thing

15. Worth the schlep suburban treat and you can go beyond Zone 3 for this one

16. You wish you'd thought of yourself admiration meets professional jealously

London's 20 Most Recommended

Le Gavroche

The Wolseley

The Greenhouse

Le Café Anglais

Scott's

Sketch

Barrafina

The Square

Royal China

St John

Umu

Hakkasan

Roka

Wild Honey

L'Atelier de Joël Robuchon

Yauatcha

Pétrus

Chez Bruce

Hix Oyster and Chophouse

The Top 5s

The 'London's 20 Most Recommended' list falls in order of the number of times each restaurant was mentioned as an answer across all 16 questions, put to the panel of industry insiders.

Below are a series of Top 5's, made up of the most popular answers for the 16 questions that were asked. It's no great surprise that The Wolseley is the most popular choice for breakfast, that Café Boheme is the Top late night choice or Cha Cha Moon the cheap choice.

Instead, perhaps the most surprising category contains the places that were felt to be 'one of a kind London experiences' with St John the most popular choice by a long way and not a pie 'n' mash shop anywhere in sight.

While the restaurant everybody admired the most and wish they'd thought of themselves – was Yauatcha.

Finally, the restaurant that ended up in the most Top 5 was Le Gavroche with four appearances, for service, which it topped, wine list, which it also topped, making an impression and when someone else is paying.

Dine solo
1. Barrafina
2. Wild Honey (Bar)
3. Bentley's (Oyster Bar)
4. J Sheekey (Oyster Bar)
5. Bibendum (Oyster Bar)

On-the-hoof
1. Ranoush Juice
2. Royal China
3. Barrafina
4. Busaba Eathai
5. Cha Cha Moon

Lazy Sunday
1. Le Café Anglais
2. Royal China
3. Electric Brasserie
4. Anchor & Hope
5. The River Café

Breakfast
1. The Wolseley
2. Cecconi's
3. St John Bread & Wine
4. Villandry
5. Lucky 7

People watch
1. The Wolseley
2. Cipriani
3. Scott's
4. Sketch
5. Nobu

Abuse the wine list
1. Le Gavroche
2. The Greenhouse
3. Vinoteca
4. Le Café Anglais
5. The Square

Clandestine rendezvous
1. Café Boheme
2. Roka (Shochu Lounge)
3. Sushi Hiro
4. St Pancras Champagne Bar
5. Traders Vics

Make an impression
1. Hakkasan
2. Le Gavroche
3. The Greenhouse
4. Scott's
5. L'Atelier de Joël Robuchon

When someone else pays
1. Le Gavroche
2. Umu
3. L'Atelier de Joël Robuchon
4. The Greenhouse
5. Zuma

Late night dining
1. Café Boheme
2. Maroush
3. Beirut Express
4. Ranoush
5. Mr Kong

Quintessential London
1. St John
2. Galvin at Windows
3. Hix Oyster and Chophouse
4. Sweetings
5. The Albemarle

Be pampered
1. Le Gavroche
2. The Greenhouse
3. The Square
4. The Albemarle
5. Chez Bruce

Frugal feasting
1. Cha Cha Moon
2. Tayyabs
3. Hung Tao
4. Japan Centre (Toku)
5. Royal China

Worth the schlep
1. Petersham Nurseries
2. La Trompette
3. Sushi Hiro
4. Sushi Say
5. Chez Bruce

Wish they'd thought of it
1. Yauatcha
2. Roka
3. Arbutus
4. Barrafina
5. L'Atelier de Joël Robuchon

Pub Grub
1. Anchor & Hope
2. Fox & Anchor
3. Anglesea Arms
4. St John's
5. The Carpenter's Arms

L'Absinthe
French

Abuse the wine list/Frugal feasting

Next time you hear some know-it-all bang on about 'doomed restaurant sites' point them to NW1's L'Absinthe, which has changed hands more times over the last decade than Primrose Hill princess Kate Moss has changed boyfriends. It's now a cute wine shop cum dining room that gives the locals (many of whom admittedly wouldn't know a good restaurant if it came up and bit them on the arse) what they want. In this case that means a familiar oh-so-French-it-almost-hurts-but-still-charming bistro that serves onion soup and duck confit. It's slickly run by Jean-Christophe Slowik, an ex Marco Pierre White major-domo for 20 years and somehow still smiling. The set lunch menu, priced

"the set lunch menu is a steal, as is the compact all-French wine list"

at £8.50 for two courses, or for one course, with a glass of wine and a coffee, is a steal, as is the compact all-French wine list.

40 Chalcot Road, Primrose Hill, NW1 8LS
Tel: 020 7483 4848 £34
Open: noon–2.30pm (4pm Sat/Sun), 4pm (6pm Sat/Sun)–10.30pm (9.30pm Sun). Closed Mondays.

The Albemarle

Be pampered/Breakfast/Quintessential London

Formerly the Grill at Brown's (and before that 1837) this fine old Mayfair hotel's restaurant has been rechristened again. With the new name came the involvement of Mark Hix (see Hix Oyster & Chophouse page 78) who installed head chef Lee Streeton and made over the menu to make it more British, more seasonal, more luxurious and no less meaty or traditional. The carving trolley is rolled out every lunch, its cargo varying from Beef

"more British, more seasonal, more luxurious"

Wellington on a Wednesday to roast beef on a Sunday. Elsewhere there are oysters, simply prepared fish dishes, on-the-bone cuts, and proper puddings. The room, restored under Rocco Forte's ownership several years ago, is all wood-panelling and plush carpet, a style that suits the service. The à la carte breakfast, that includes helpings of kedgeree and kippers, is affordable, unlike the, traditionally priced for a 5-star-hotel, full English.

Brown's Hotel, Albemarle Street, Mayfair, W1S 4BP
Tel: 020 7493 6020   www.brownshotel.com   £53
Open: 7–10.30am, noon–3pm, 5.30–11pm Mon–Sat;
7.30–11am, 12.30–3pm, 7–10.30pm Sun

Anchor & Hope

Modern British

Pub grub/Lazy Sunday

An economically tarted-up 70s boozer sat in the shade
of a Southwark council block, serving gutsy seasonal
cooking. The tersely written menu, which changes twice
a day, has shades of St John (see page 133) about it with
a love of offal, big bits of beast and rustic simplicity –
not surprising really as one of the founding chefs
worked there back in the day. Shared dishes, such as
slow-cooked stuffed duck, regularly appear on the blackboard for two, four or six. The service can on occasion

seem slightly stoned
but is always smiley.
The Monday–Satur-

*" a love of offal, big bits of
beast and rustic simplicity"*

day no-reservations policy still pisses off those who
can't be bothered to turn up early or don't fancy booking
a table for their set one-seating Sunday lunch. The same
team has since tweaked their winning formula with
Great Queen Street (see page 72) to open in the West
End.

36 The Cut, Southwark, SE1 8LP
Tel: 020 7928 9898   £32
Open: noon–2.30pm, 6–10.30pm Tues–Sat; 12.30–5pm Sun

Andrew Edmunds

Map C

Modern British

Abuse the wine list/Clandestine rendezvous

This popular scruffy Soho institution is named after the legendarily cantankerous owner of the adjacent antiquarian print gallery. Edmunds annexed what was a Dutch wine bar, where he liked to sit and eat his lunch everyday, when it went bust back in the 80s. Under his ownership it offers quality helpings of classy, well-executed, simple seasonal comfort food, like the best gas-

"classy, well-executed, simple seasonal comfort food"

tropub grub but better. Candlelit at night, it's regularly name-checked as one of London's most romantic tables, although those who do so probably sit upstairs in the comparatively capacious but still cosy ground floor dining room, as opposed to the beyond bijou basement. You'll need to book to bag a table and, irritatingly, they only take reservations seven days in advance. The service is pleasingly spunky and the well-assembled wine list is big on choice and low on mark-ups.

46 Lexington Street, Soho, W1R 3LH
Tel: 020 7437 5708   £34
Open: daily, noon (1pm Sat)–3pm, 6–10.30pm (10.45pm Sat)

Angelus

French

Abuse the wine list/Clandestine rendezvous

Not much is left to remind you that this was once The Archway Tavern save the stained-glass window of a Robin Hood-type. Tucked behind Lancaster Gate it reopened as this rather plush brasserie last year; red leather banquettes and Art Nouveau-style mirrors com-

bining nicely with the original high ceilings, dark carved wooden-panelling and iron

"brasserie deluxe dishes such as his now trademark foie gras brûlée"

staircase. Although some sad sods no doubt lament the passing of what was previously a bog standard boozer, the locals should be pleased with Angelus' arrival in an area that's not exactly generously blessed with decent restaurants. Thierry Thomasin, previously head somme-lier at Le Gavroche (see page 71) and latterly of Aubergine, runs the rather polished show here with chef Olivier Duret turning out brasserie deluxe dishes such as his now trademark foie gras *brûlée*. The wine list, as you'd expect considering Thomasin's CV, does not disap-point.

4 Bathurst Street, Lancaster Gate, W2 2SD
Tel: 020 7402 0083   www.angelusrestaurant.com   £42
Open: 11am–midnight. Closed Mondays.

Anglesea Arms

Modern British

Pub grub

In a world now inhabited by so many ho-hum 'gastropubs', this neighbourhood boozer has been delivering
since around about the time the term was first coined.
It's been through a few changes in ownership and chef
since then but this compact corner pub has rightly man-

aged to keep its
reputation for af-
fordable, gutsy,
seasonal cooking.
The menu,
scrawled on a
blackboard each
day, usually has
half a dozen or so
starters and
mains, and several
puds. You can't
make reservations,
service can be
slack, and it's filled
with the usual
mismatched furni-
ture. There's a
separate dining
area but the menu,
which usually
finds space for

*"has rightly managed to keep its
reputation for affordable gutsy
seasonal cooking"*

oysters, seasonal salads, simply grilled fish and a decent
number of meaty options, is available throughout.
There's a good selection of real ale behind the bar, while
the wine list is surprisingly grand in places.

35 Wingate Road, Hammersmith, W6 0UR
Tel: 020 8749 1292   £35
Open: daily, noon–11pm (10.30pm Sun)

L'Anima

Italian

Abuse the wine list/Make an impression

This recently opened modern Italian, a hop, skip and a jump from Liverpool Street Station, if you go the right way, has already made a big impact on the City crowd. But it's simply too good to just serve the suits. Housed in a shiny glass-fronted ground floor of the site of a spanking new Broadgate office building, it's been decked out in a very sparse mini-malist fashion and is staffed front of house by hand-some, efficient, smiley sorts. The wine list has the usual famous Ital-ian names along-side some pleas-ingly obscure va-rieties and blends.

"a combination of comfort, rustic touches and simply grilled meat and fish"

But it's the menu overseen by chef-proprietor Francesco Mazzei that steals the show with a combination of com-fort, rustic touches and simply grilled meat and fish. Sweet teeth are rewarded with exemplary desserts such as liquorice *zabayon* & *croccantino* ice cream.

1 Snowden Street, Shoreditch, EC2A 2DQ
Tel: 020 7422 7000 www.lanima.co.uk   £54
Open: 7–10.30am, 11.45am–3pm, 5.30–10.30pm Mon–Fri

Apollo Banana Leaf

Frugal feasting/On-the-hoof

Not somewhere to be approached with a raging hangover, if only because of the disconcerting combination of canned music, mirrors and crap ethnic art, this simple café in Tooting is a destination for local Tamil families who only pay attention to the affordable Sri Lankan cooking. The Sri Lankan specialities share space on the menu with north Indian dishes. But it's the southern subcontinent seafood dishes such as fish cutlets, crab curry and squid curry – at if not quite authentic Sri Lankan prices, as close as you'll get anywhere in London – that are more worthy of investigation.

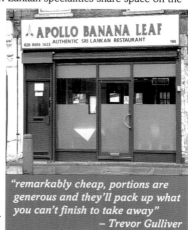

"remarkably cheap, portions are generous and they'll pack up what you can't finish to take away"
— *Trevor Gulliver*

Trevor Gulliver, the restaurateur behind St John, a fan, says, 'It's remarkably cheap, portions are generous and they'll pack up what you can't finish to take away.' Its unlicensed but there's no charge for corkage and a surfeit of nearby off- licences.

190 Tooting High Street, Tooting, SW17 0SF
Tel: 020 8696 1423   £16
Open: noon–3pm, 6–11pm Mon–Weds; noon–11pm
Thurs–Sun

Map
C

Arbutus
Modern British

Abuse the wine list/Wish they'd thought of it

Such has been its success since it opened early in the summer of 2006 that it's already become unfashionable to praise Soho's Arbutus. Anthony Demetre's pared down plates of French food often make use of cheaper cuts that are brightened by his technical prowess. Dishes such as squid and mackerel burger, the kitchen's way

with a saddle of rabbit and the sweet relief found

"cheaper cuts are brightened by his technical prowess"

in *claufoutis* for afters keep the punters coming. Meanwhile Will Smith's ruse of offering every bottle of a compact but well-chosen wine list by the glass and 250ml carafe (an idea he picked up on a trip to New York) likewise garnered almost universal plaudits. Accessible and affordable, the dining room is simply designed and informal, the service always warm and professional. They've since swiftly repeated the same trick over in Mayfair with Wild Honey (see page 158).

63–64 Frith Street, Soho, W1D 3JW
Tel: 020 7734 4545 www.arbutusrestaurant.co.uk   £38
Open: daily, noon–2.30pm, 5–10.30pm; 12.30–3.30pm, 5.30–9.30pm Sun

Assaggi

Be pampered/When someone else pays

A long-running local hero to the well-heeled residents of Notting Hill and Bayswater, critical praise, including a stellar rating from the guide bankrolled by a French tyre manufacturer, brings destination diners – some of whom don't understand what all the fuss is about. The small dining room, unpromisingly perched above the

"simple but accomplished Italian cooking"

Chepstow pub, is nothing much to look at, brightly painted with furniture that looks like it's been foraged from some rustic classroom. But it's a battle to secure one of its only 11 tables. The forthright but friendly service makes everyone – loyal regulars and newcomers alike – feel special. Everything's confidently declared '*bellisimo*' as you order it and when it arrives at the table, simple but accomplished Italian cooking made with the sort of ingredients that don't come cheap (something reflected in the bill), everything is indeed most beautiful.

39 Chepstow Place, Notting Hill, W2 4TS
Tel: 020 7792 9033 £67
Open: 12.30 (1pm Sat)–11pm. Closed Sundays.

Atari-Ya

Japanese

Frugal feasting/On-the-hoof

The words 'cheap' and 'sushi' are rarely seen together in the same sentence and when they are it's more than likely in reference to somewhere other than the London's West End – or a warning to eat elsewhere at all costs. Atari-Ya just off Oxford Street is a rare exception providing quality bargain basement sushi and *sashimi* by virtue of the fact that its parent company is a Japanese fish wholesaler that supplies many of London's sushi restaurants. Also available are simple cooked dishes such as *una don*, grilled eel coated in a sweet sauce and

"quality bargain basement sushi and sashimi"

served over rice. Unlicensed (grab a weird and wonderful Japanese soft drink instead) it's laid out like a cramped deli where you can, in theory, eat in by somehow grabbing one of a handful seats but Jason Atherton, head chef of Maze, swears by their takeaway.

20 James Street, Marylebone, W1U 1EH
Tel: 020 7491 1178 www.atariya.co.uk   £12
Open: daily, 11am–8pm

L'Atelier de Joël Robuchon French

Map
C

Wish they'd thought of it/Dine solo/Make an impression/When someone else pays

From the chef with the mostly highly rated collection of restaurants on the planet, the London branch of L'Atelier looks very much like those Joël Robuchon has opened everywhere from Tokyo to Las Vegas in the last

few years. The ground floor is a low-lit combination of black and red that makes it look like a giant bento box at battle with a 80s cocktail bar. Customers sit along a sleek shiny counter and eat small plates of some of possibly the most exquisite seasonal modern French cooking currently in London. Upstairs is the more formal dinner-only La Cuisine de

"possibly the most exquisite seasonal modern French cooking currently in London"

Joël Robuchon and Le Salon Bar. Keep it downstairs if you're watching your wallet where, unless you somehow have the resolve to leave after a quick steak tartare with retro crinkle cut chips and a glass of wine, it can still get expensive.

13 West Street, Covent Garden, WC2H 9NE
Tel: 020 7010 8600 www.joel-robuchon.com   £73
Open: daily, noon–3pm, 5.30–11pm (10.30pm Sun)

Bar Asia

Asian

Clandestine rendezvous/On-the-hoof

A newcomer to South Kensington on the Old Brompton Road site that previously housed the coffee, papers and cakes, Café News. Despite calling itself something that supposedly aspires to a pan Asian menu, the food tends to focus on the Indian subcontinent and only drops in elsewhere in Asia for a spot of *dim sum*, stir-fry and *yakitori* in among the selection of *samosas*, curries, tandoori dishes and *biryanis*. The ground floor is a bijou, blue-lit bar with smart black leather banquettes that serves a good line in cocktails such as watermelon martinis, that go down rather well with the Asian finger-food. Below

stairs lies the main dining room that, depending on trade, tends to only open in the evening.

"Cosy, dark-walled and candle-lit, it's worth seeking out for those conducting secret trysts"

Cosy, dark-walled and candle-lit, it's worth seeking out for those conducting secret trysts or suffering from severe light sensitivity.

166 Old Brompton Road, Earl's Court, SW5 0BA
Tel: 020 7373 2626   £34
Open: noon–3pm, 6–10.45pm. Closed Sundays.

Bar Shu

Sichuan

Map
C

Frugal feasting/Make an impression

Soho Sichuanese with a menu put together with the help
of Fuchsia Dunlop, a respected British cookery writer
specialising in Chinese food and author of *Sichuan Cookery*, that's paved the way for newcomers such as Snazz
Sichuan (see page 129). Sichuan vir-
gins would do best to gen-up a bit be-
forehand because despite Dunlop's
erudite efforts and the (thankfully un-
flattering) food-photography there's
mystery in the menu for the uninitiated, an aw-
ful lot of offal and dishes that don't make an appearance at the average Chinese, such as flower-explod-
ing kidneys and husband and wife offal. Be aware of
the use of mind-numbing amounts of Sichuan pepper and hefty helpings
of chilli in some dishes that might mean that you tem-
porarily lose your sense of taste. Accept that and the
fact that the service can sometimes be slipshod and enjoy the fiery trip.

*"Be aware of the use of mind-
numbing amounts of Sichuan
pepper and hefty helpings of
chilli"*

28 Frith Street, Soho, W1D 5LF
Tel: 020 7287 8822 www.bar-shu.co.uk
Open: daily, noon–11.30pm

£45

Map
C

Barrafina

Spanish

Abuse the wine list/Dine solo/On-the-hoof/ Wish they'd thought of it

The Anglo-Iberian Hart brothers' follow up to the well-regarded Fino in Charlotte Street, Barrafina is their tribute to Barcelona's legendary Cal Pep. It produces top class tapas from Jabugo, *tortilla* et al via helpings of grilled meat and game to seafood cooked *a la plancha*,

all of which somehow finds its way from the crammed

"The food is ably supplemented by an excellent all-Iberian selection of wines and good-natured service"

open kitchen behind the bar. The food is ably supplemented by an excellent all-Iberian selection of wines and good-natured service. Some still find the no-reservations policy for the 23-stools around the marble counter irksome in the extreme but either you're prepared to grab a draught of cold Cruzcampo or two and a plate of *jamon*, while you wait and watch Soho go by – or you're not. Those in the vicinity can now check out the length of the line via live webcam from their website.

54 Frith Street, Soho, W1D 4SL
Tel: 020 7813 8016 www.barrafina.co.uk   £58
Open: daily, noon–3pm, 5–11pm Mon-Sat; 12.30–3.30pm, 5.30–10.30pm Sun

Beigel Bake

Late night/People Watch/On-the-hoof

Beloved East End institution that's open 24 hours-a-day, 7 days-a-week. Although it gets especially busy when it's chucking out time for the pubs and clubs, a visit at breakfast or lunchtime is just as likely to end up with you queuing. But it's a multisensory treat, particularly in the small hours, from the sight of worse-for-wear club-bers and local characters to the sweet smell of baking

"the sweet smell of baking overpowers the many more unpleasant scents wafting along Brick Lane"

that overpowers the many more unpleasant scents wafting along Brick Lane. The shop it-self doesn't look like it's been refitted since the 60s. The bagels – or more properly beigels – are freshly boiled and baked on the premises and are smaller than the im-ported American variety you find in the supermarket. Al-so available plain, they're filled with slabs of salt beef, heaps of herring or an abundance of cream cheese and salmon. For afters, the cakes are just as generously pro-portioned.

159 Brick Lane, Shoreditch, E1 6SB
Tel: 020 7729 0616   £3
Open: daily, 24 hours

Beirut Express Lebanese

Breakfast/Dine solo/Late night/On-the-hoof

This part of the Maroush massive, like its various siblings along the Middle Eastern enclave that is Edgware Road, is a livelier location when the sun goes down than it is during the day. That said, the ever popular Beirut Express, a favourite on-the-hoof haunt of Mourad 'Momo' Mazouz,

which serves good quality *meze*, chargrilled meats, *shawarma*, salads and the usual fine selection of freshly made fruit juices until the small hours, is much less of a nocturnal beast than many of its neighbouring cafés and restaurants. Open every day for breakfast from 7am, when if you're feeing fragile you can hunker down and work out how you're going to face the

"quality meze, char-grilled meats, salads and the usual fine selection of freshly made fruit juices until the small hours"

world with a Lebanese coffee, so strong and thick that you can almost stand a teaspoon up in it, and some scrambled eggs served with homemade spicy beef sausage.

112–114 Edgware Road, Marylebone, W2 2DZ
Tel: 020 7724 2700 www.maroush.com   £38
Open: daily, 7am–2am

Benares

When someone else pays/Make an impression /Be pampered

Atul Kochhar has got form when it comes to doing May-fair-Indian-deluxe. Formerly head chef of the nearby Tamarind (see page 140) he opened Benares, overlooking Berkeley Square, in 2003. Reassuringly (or is that predictably?) expensive, it's a chic windowless palace of

top-notch modern Indian hospitality. The flavours achieved, particularly with the *tandoor*, are exceptional. Elsewhere there's an occasional touch of fusion on display in dishes which incorporate European ingredients, such as foie gras. For those who want a no-expense-spared experience there's the multi-coursed grazing menu with wine flight. That Kochhar has maintained stand-

"a chic windowless palace of top-notch modern Indian hospitality"

dards, in the flagship of a nascent empire now, is a compliment to Benares' brigade. Front of house is a smooth but far from speedy operation, one that deals best with customers that who to luxuriate in a haute Indian experience.

12 Berkeley Square House, Mayfair, W1J 6BS
Tel: 020 7629 8886   www.benaresrestaurant.com   £64
Open: noon–2.30pm, 5.30–11pm Mon–Sat; 6–10.30pm Sun

Bentley's

Seafood

Dine solo/Wish they'd thought of it

The most English of restaurants dating back to 1916, Bentley's has been reborn since it fell into the hands of an Irishman back in 2005. Richard Corrigan's refurbishment of this classic West End oyster bar and grill, where he worked as head chef back in the early 90s, has restored its once stellar reputation for shellfish and seafood. Upstairs lies the Grill with its meatier menu featuring West Cork beef. But it's the cosier more informal champagne bar, drinking accompanied by a pianist most evenings, and the adjacent shellfish-focused ground-floor oyster bar, where marble counter meets red leather upholstery and seasoned old oyster campaigners in white jackets do their shucking, that feels particularly special. Outside a large swathe of Swallow Street has been given over to Bentley's for al fresco dining in the warmer weather.

"Richard Corrigan's refurbishment... has restored its once stellar reputation for shellfish and seafood"

11–15 Swallow Street, Piccadilly, W1B 4DG
Tel: 020 7734 4756   www.bentleys.org   £47
Oyster bar: daily, noon–midnight (Sun 10pm)
Grill: noon–3pm, 6–11pm Mon–Sat; 11.30am–3.30pm, 6–10pm Sun

Best Turkish Kebab

Turkish

Frugal feasting/On-the-hoof/Late night

That name makes quite a claim – since there are an ungodly number of Turkish kebab shops in N16 alone – never mind London. But no other than the great trencherman Charles Campion, of *The Evening Standard* and *The London Restaurant Guide*, backs up its veracity. He declares this busy 'distinguished kebab shop' in Stoke Newington his takeaway of choice for their doners, made from shoulder meat, with just the right spicing

"These are doners that... still taste great stone cold sober"

and no additives. These are doners that, unlike many pitiful examples on offer elsewhere, still taste great stone cold sober. The kebab shop in question also happens to be wonderfully well run, with a crew of eight kebab assemblers behind the counter at busy times to keep the line moving, is spotlessly clean and a civilised place that thoughtfully offers you wet wipes for use after your well-packed pita.

125 Stoke Newington Road, Dalston, N16 8BT
Tel: 020 7254 7642   £7
Open: daily, 11am–2am

Bibendum

French

Dine solo/Make an impression

Michelin's British headquarters from 1909 to 1985, this striking Art Nouveau landmark was reborn in 1987 as an upmarket eating destination courtesy of designer, restaurateur and retailer Terence Conran, filmmaker Michael Hamlyn and chef Simon Hopkinson. The Edwardian building with its overstated stained-glass windows, showing the famous tyre-man at play, is as striking as it ever was. In addition to the main restaurant and oyster bar, it also houses a café and a crustacean stall. The ground floor oyster bar, which doesn't take reservations, has one of the best selections of bivalve molluscs in London, while upstairs, in the more grown-up restaurant, head chef Matthew Harris, brother of Henry Harris of Racine (see page 115) oversees an upmarket but easy to get along with French menu, with an occasional bit of British comfort, such as deep-fried haddock and chips, thrown in.

"The ground floor oyster bar... has one of the best selections of bi-valve molluscs in London"

81 Fulham Road, South Kensington, SW3 6RD
Tel: 020 7581 5817 www.bibendum.co.uk   £59
Open: noon (12.30pm Sat/Sun)–2.30pm (3pm Sat/Sun),
7–11pm (10.30pm Sun) Oyster bar: daily, noon–11pm

Bistrotheque

People watch/Lazy Sunday/Worth the schlep

Less a restaurant, more a streetwise arty scene with camp cabaret (is there any other sort?) in a tiled Hackney warehouse space that serves accomplished French inflected comfort food. That the gay bingo and the like don't completely overshadow the menu, where cheese-

"more than worth the journey to 'the badlands of Bethnal Green"

burgers and half a roast chicken sit easily alongside charcuterie and crab cakes served with a grapefruit hollandaise, shows that the kitchen knows how to keep its audience happy. For Jennifer Sharp, editor and restaurant critic, it's more than worth the journey to, "the badlands of Bethnal Green… for being on the doorstep of the edgy art galleries on Vyner Street and environs" and its "sparkling owners". Popular with the fashion crowd, it's only open in the evenings, except at weekends when they serve brunch and Sunday lunch – the latter accompanied by an artiste on the baby grand.

23–27 Wadeson Street, Hackney, E2 9DR
Tel: 020 8983 7900 www.bistrotheque.com   £43
Open: daily, 6pm (1pm Sun)–midnight

Blueprint Café Modern British

**Abuse the wine list/Quintessential London/
Worth the schlep**

Smart seasonal British cooking from evergreen Scot Jeremy Lee with a very fine view, across the Thames from its glazed terrace that takes in the Tower Bridge, the Tower of London and the Gherkin, thrown in. They're kind enough to include a pair of disposable binoculars on the table to allow diners to make the most of their enviable vantage point. The Blueprint celebrates 20 years on the first floor of Design Museum come 2009. Lee has cooked there since 1989 and takes an accomplished but unfussy approach in a daily-changing menu that takes inspiration and ingredients from his native Scotland, particularly in the colder months, and Eu-

"an accomplished but unfussy approach... that takes inspiration and ingredients from his native Scotland"

rope throughout the year. Lee's way with game is especially worth the journey. Formerly every sane diner's favourite Conran dining room, it's currently the thinking restaurant-goers pick of the rechristened D&D London stable.

Design Museum, 28 Shad Thames, Southwark, SE1 2YD
Tel: 020 7378 7031 www.danddlondon.com £42
Open: noon–3pm, 6–11pm Mon–Fri; noon–11pm Sat; noon–10.30pm Sun

Bodeans

Dine solo/On-the-hoof

The original Soho branch of Bodean's is set over two floors, the ground floor given over to a take away/deli setup and downstairs to tartan-carpeted, mostly boothed, restaurant with peppy service and antler horn lamps. Happily standards have not slipped since the re-

"Sod the not-so-special starters and instead pig-out on the mains"

cent opening of three other branches in south, west and east London and this remains Bodean's mothership. Sod the not-so-special starters and instead pig-out on the mains: slabs of ribs (baby back or spare), pulled pork (also served as sandwich in soft white roll and called a 'Boston Butt') and the occasional pleasure of 'Burnt Ends' (slow smoked bites of beef brisket, which are only available on Mondays and Wednesdays) all of which are served with coleslaw and BBQ beans. Home to homesick Americans glued to odd sports on the 42" plasma screen and hungry Soho types.

16 D'Arblay Street, Soho, W1F 8PZ
Tel: 020 7287 0506 www.bodeansbbq.com   £34
Open: daily, noon–3pm, 6–11pm, noon–11pm (10.30pm Sun) Sat/Sun

Boiled Egg & Soldiers British

Breakfast

While this Battersea breakfast and brunch joint has the right sort of menu for soaking up a hangover, its popularity with the area's masses of smug yummy-mummery and their perfect little princesses (typically named after emotions, countries and water movements) and princes (usually called Tom, Dick or Harry) can jar – even if you don't have a throbbing alcohol-induced headache. Which could explain the occasionally indifferent service. One coping strategy of course is to keep drinking and happily this is one breakfast joint with a full licence. So there's no rea-

"numb the pain and grab a Bloody Mary or two or a bottle of champagne with... a full fry-up"

son why you can't numb the pain and grab a Bloody Mary or two or a bottle of Champagne with everything from a full fry-up to the eponymous house special via smoked haddock or the hefty helping of bacon, sirloin steak and black pudding that they call 'The Works'.

63 Northcote Road, Clapham, SW11 1NP
Tel: 020 7223 4894 £14
Open: daily, 9am–6pm (4.30pm Sun)

Brasserie St Jacques

Dine solo

Recently opened French brasserie on St James's site that's changed its frontage frequently, around four times in the last four years, since it saw action as the original home of Pétrus (see page 107). Nothing's been decon-

"the sort of honest brasserie you'll find in any French city"

structed here, it's the sort of honest brasserie that you'd find in any French city, and for those burnt out on reinvented bourgeois French, all the better for it. The interior with its mustard-yellow walls and paper place mat topped tables is unre- markable; this, af- ter all, is a neigh- bourhood restau- rant, albeit for a very expensive neighbourhood. The menu was put together by London haute cuisine legend Pierre Koff- man, who pulls no surprises with a long list of classics from garlic snails and foie gras terrine to salade niçoise and *coq au vin*. Desserts are equally familiar fail-safes such as lemon tart and rum baba.

33 St James' Street, Mayfair, SW1A 7HD
Tel: 020 7839 1007   www.brasseriestjacques.co.uk   £46
Open: daily, 8am (9am Sun)–11pm (10pm Sun)

Map

C

Busaba Eathai

Thai

Dine solo/Frugal feasting/On-the-hoof/Wish they'd thought of it

That the original Soho branch of Alan Yau's intelligent Thai canteen, which opened back in 1999, still has fast-moving queues outside it on Friday and Saturday nights, speaks in part of its warm welcoming dark-wooden design. It's also about the accessible, affordable menu, originally put together by David Thompson of Nahm, that has enough quality Thai staples to keep the com-

"Low-lit, shared, square teak-stained tables create a convivial vibe"

fort-eaters happy while pushing the envelope elsewhere with an ever-evolving line-up of new dishes. There's a healthy slant to much of the menu, particularly the salads, and although there is beer, wine, sake and cocktails available, the soft drinks menu contains such soothing elixirs as hot lemongrass and honey. Low-lit, shared, square teak-stained tables create a convivial vibe, although the bare, wooden, low-slung benches make for a numb arse if you sit much beyond the half-hour mark.

106–110 Wardour Street, Soho, W1F 0TS
Tel: 020 7255 8686 www.busaba.com   £31
Open: daily, noon–11pm (11.30pm Fri/Sat, 10pm Sun)

Byron

Dine solo/On-the-hoof

This, the first branch of this bright branded 'new burger' bar, by the side of Holland Park on Kensington High Street, where Giles Coren recommends you eat on the fly, has immediately made an impact in what's now a crowded field, what with Gourmet Burger Kitchen, Ultimate Burger, The Fine Burger Co. and Hamburger Union. Designed around a central grill with stools, banquettes, cutesy murals and a colour scheme that's a white-washed diner with splashes of pastel. The burgers are made from trace-able grass-fed cattle, minced daily and char-grilled. They'll even cook them rare for you, if that's how you like your burger,

"They'll even cook them rare for you... which shows they're sure of the quality of their Aberdeen Angus beef"

which shows they're sure of the quality of their Aberdeen Angus beef. The baps are soft and white and the chips, shoestring or the hand-cut variety. They also do nice things like frost your glass if you order a beer. Families and shoppers pack it out at the weekend.

222 Kensington High Street, Kensington, W8 7RG
Tel: 020 7361 1717 www.byronhamburgers.com   £25
Open: daily, noon (11am Sat/Sun)–11pm (11.30pm Fri/Sat, 10.30pm Sun)

Le Café Anglais Anglo-French

Abuse the wine list/Lazy Sunday/People watch/Wish they'd thought of it

This recent transformation of a particularly unloved branch of McDonald's into a handsome British brasserie turns out to have been a masterstroke and something that both Nick Jones of Soho House and Fay Maschler wish they'd thought of. Sure it's on the second floor of a currently uninspiring mall but the separate entrance, with its own lift, means you can sidestep the shoppers.

Although the service is still finding its feet, Rowley Leigh (ex of Kensington

"a vast menu of classy comfort food that's not afraid to be French"

Place, where they seem to be missing him) has crafted a vast menu of classy comfort food that's not afraid to be French. Neither is his impressive New World-shunning wine list. The pleasingly retro *hors d'oeuvres* selection, including the much eulogized Parmesan custard and anchovy toasts, is a fine way to start a meal. Simple fish dishes and rotisserie-roasted meat and game make up the mains and desserts veer from simple fresh fruit to rib-sticking nostalgia.

8 Porchester Gardens, Bayswater, W2 4DB
Tel: 020 7721 1415 www.lecafeanglais.co.uk £50
Open: daily, noon–3.30pm, 6.30–11pm

Café Bohème

Breakfast/Clandestine rendezvous/Late night/People watch

'

This bustling Old Compton Street mainstay, opened back in 1992, has recently been bought and remade partly in the image of the other Soho House brasseries, such as the Electric, but is much more French in look and feel. Replete with burgundy leather banquettes and a zinc-topped bar, it's open all day from breakfast until the wee hours. The menu, which is the work of Henry

"After midnight the pared menu still includes fish soup, oysters, duck confit and chocolate mousse"

Harris who has since returned to Racine (see page 115), runs through the usual French classics cum clichés, from *croque monsieur* to *tarte tatin* via a rather good *steak frites*. After midnight the pared menu still includes fish soup, oysters, duck *confit* and chocolate mousse. The basement hides the plush invite-only lounge bar, Boheme's so-called 'salon'. Full of hidden alcoves crying out for secret assignations, it's well worth flirting with the management to gain access.

13–17 Old Compton Street, Soho, W1D 5GD

Tel: 020 7734 0623   www.cafeboheme.co.uk   £37
Open: daily, 7.30am (8am Sat/Sun)–3am (midnight Sun)

The Capital

Anglo-French

Clandestine rendezvous/Make an impression/Quintessential London

Legendary dining room in a famous old Knightsbridge hotel thats serves as the most unassuming haute destination in town. Head chef Eric Chavot is one of London's most consistently excellent performers. A champion of British ingredients and an accomplished practitioner of fine French technique, he uses both in combinations such as home cured 'treacle' salmon with deep-fried soft shell crab and pan-fried foie gras with cherry and pistachio crumble. Every thing else is as it should be. The wine list is hefty, the service formal and the

"A champion of British ingredients and an accomplished practitioner of fine French tech-

dining room slightly dull but luxuriously comfortable. It's, as you might imagine, an expensive restaurant, but the three-course set lunch at £29.50 makes it manageable.

22–24 Basil Street, Knightsbridge, SW3 1AT
Tel: 020 7589 5171 www.capitalhotel.co.uk   £79
Open: daily, noon–2.30pm, 6.45–10pm

Le Caprice

Clandestine rendezvous/Dine solo/Make an impression/People watch/Wish they'd thought of it

Having celebrated its 50th birthday not so long ago, Le Caprice is one of London's longest running restaurant success stories. Its modern revival, the work of Chris

"eat at the bar, be very well looked after and watch the regulars"

Corbin and Jeremy King, pitched its interior as 80s Manhattan chic and it's stayed pretty much that way ever since. The menu wanders all over Europe but mostly looks to Italy and Britain before ending up in somewhere near Sweden for dessert with their, now classic, Scandinavian ice berries served with hot white chocolate sauce. You can eat at the bar, be very well looked after and watch the regulars, who still number assorted socialites and celebs, despite the many upstart establishments that have come along since 1981. The service is friendly and professional but slick to the point of being hurried if you're not someone, and it's still a bugger to get a reservation.

Arlington House, Mayfair, SW1A 1RJ
Tel: 020 7629 2239 www.le-caprice.co.uk   £52
Open: daily, noon–3pm (5pm Sun), 5.30pm–midnight (11pm Sun)

The Carpenter's Arms
British

Pub grub/Lazy Sunday

This simple grub pub just off Hammersmith's King Street is touted by locals and *Metro's* restaurant critic Marina O'Loughlin as offering healthy competition to the nearby Anglesea Arms (see page 17). "Brilliant – textbook stuff: good bread, stout flavours, sussed cooking, first-class ingredients, mellow atmosphere," gushes O'Loughlin, "Great pics of The Sweeney, too." The kitchen, run by chef Paul Adams (formerly of The Pig's Ear, see page 110), serves up a short, smart menu of an appropriately seasonal line of robust British food with a few foreign flourishes, such as Tuscan chestnut soup, steamed razor clams with parsley, garlic and cream, salt-beef sandwich with beetroot and pickles, and poacher's pie, amply stuffed with game birds. The dining room

"textbook stuff: good bread, stout flavours, sussed cooking, first-class ingredients, mellow atmosphere" – Marina O'Loughlin

is plain but attractively decorated and, there's a pleasant little courtyard where you can outside when it's warmer, and the Sunday lunch is cracking.

91 Black Lion Lane, Hammersmith, W6 9BG
Tel: 020 8741 8386
£35
Open: daily, noon–11pm

Le Cassoulet

French

Worth the schlep

There are those who wax lyrical about Croydon's unique collection of roundabouts, concrete skyline and the fact Kate Moss was born there. But beyond that the south London suburb tends to get short shrift. While chef Malcom John's recently opened Le Cassoulet won't change that, at least no one can now say that Croydon has not got a fine French bistro. Marina O'Loughlin, *Metro*'s

"continuing his love affair with rustic French cooking"
– Marina O'Loughlin

restaurant critic, praises it as somewhere worth the journey, where John (who also runs Le Vacherin in Chiswick) "is continuing his love affair with rustic French bistro cooking". The interior is boudoir-on-a-budget charming, while the menu is mostly well-trodden stuff – steak tartare for starters, a signature dish of *cassoulet* for mains and *île flottante* for afters. But despite that it's not a case of familiarity breeding contempt, as each is an accomplished example of a classic.

18 Selsdon Road, Croydon, CR2 6PA
Tel: 020 8633 1818   www.lecassoulet.co.uk   £43
Open: daily, noon–3pm, 6–10pm

Cecconi's   Italian

Breakfast/Dine solo/People watch

What was once a rather stuffy, if accomplished, Mayfair Italian, first opened in 1978, and a onetime favourite of such luminaries as the Duke of Golf, was recast several years back by Nick 'Soho House' Jones as an elegant, all-day joint with a tiled floor and *prosecco* on draught. The locals, including the crew from the nearby Cork Street galleries, still seem to love it. The all day à la

carte menu covers all the usual Italian

"an elegant all-day joint with a tiled floor and prosecco on draught"

bases, some admittedly better than others. You can eat at the bar where they'll slice you some ham from the haunch on display, give you a bowl of plump olives with your drink and they know how to mix a decent cocktail. It also provides a more than decent alternative to The Wolseley (see page 159) for weekday breakfast and brunch at the weekends.

5 Burlington Gardens, Mayfair, W1X 1LE
Tel: 020 7434 1500 www.cecconis.co.uk   £57
Open: daily, 7am (8am Sat/Sun)–1am (midnight Sun)

Cha Cha Moon

Frugal feasting/On-the-hoof/Wish they'd thought of it

Alan Yau's return to the fast and hip noodle bar formula, which first won him recognition with Wagamama, tackles Chinese as opposed to Japanese noodles. All dishes have been priced at £3.50 since this, the first branch in a planned chain, opened in the summer of 2008. Yau plans to keep it that way as long as possible, making it a

"noodle dishes from Hong Kong, Sichuan and Taiwan as well as Singapore, Malaysia and Penang"

bargain. The menu takes a Pan-Chinese approach to noodles with soup and pan-fried noodle dishes from Hong Kong, Sichuan and Taiwan as well as Singapore, Malaysia and Penang. The canteen-style seating is upholstered (an improvement on both Wagamama and Busaba Eathai (see page 38), the service, slightly scattershot at times and the soft drink list (don't panic they also have booze) trawls the globe and comes back with salty lemon Sprite, Calpico, Afri Cola, Chinoto and Vitasoy malt.

15–21 Ganton Street, Soho, W1F 9BN
Tel: 020 7297 9800   £24
Open: daily, noon–11pm (11.30pm Fri/Sat, 10pm Sun)

Chez Bruce

Modern French

Abuse the wine list/Be pampered/Make an impression/Wish they'd thought of it/Worth the schlep

This, still the finest restaurant in South London, has quietly prospered on the edge of Wandsworth Common since 1995. Much like its famed precursor on the same site, Marco Pierre White's Harvey's, Chez Bruce has become a destination for off duty chefs – but don't let that put you off. Bruce Poole's refined yet unfussy French cooking is the main draw here, coming in at £25.50 for a

three-course weekday lunch and rising to £40

"Poole's cooking is nicely complemented by a welcoming dining room, fine service and a hefty wine list"

(plus supplements for when they lay on the luxury ingredients) for a three-course dinner. Poole's cooking is nicely complemented by a welcoming dining room, fine service and a hefty wine list that, in addition to seducing those with deeper pockets, features a fair share of bottles under £30. Having Chez Bruce on their doorstep perhaps explains in part why the locals all look so smug.

2 Bellevue Road, Wandsworth, SW17 7EG
Tel: 020 8672 0114   www.chezbruce.co.uk   £49
Open: noon–2pm, 6.30–10.30pm Mon–Fri; 12.30–2.30pm,
6.30–10.30pm Sat; noon–3pm, 7–10pm Sun

China Tang

Clandestine rendezvous/Make an impression/People watch/When someone else pays

The London outpost of David 'Shanghai Tang' Tang, the Asian cigar-magnate who, as well as running his upmarket international clothing label, has China Clubs in Hong Kong, Beijing and Singapore. China Tang in the bowels of The Dorchester on Park Lane is an attempt to bring a similarly upscale Cantonese experience to London. Although not quite the freak-show on display at the Cipriani, chef Adam Byatt enjoys watching the clientele, a

"The Cantonese cooking... is probably the best in town"

mixture of botox-casualties and mon-eyed younger glamour. The Cantonese cooking in dishes such as fried crispy-skin chicken, steamed sea bass and Peking duck doesn't come cheap but with Hakkasan (see page 75) and Royal China (see page 122) it's probably the best in town. The wine list starts high and goes up from there. The interior, and in particularly the bar, does a good line in 1920s Shanghai-style glamour.

The Dorchester, Park Lane, Mayfair, W1K 1QA
Tel: 020 7629 8888 www.chinatanglondon.co.uk   £52
Open: daily, 11am–3.30pm (4pm Sat/Sun), 5.30pm–midnight

49

Map C

Chinese Experience

Cantonese

Frugal feasting

This Shaftsbury Avenue Chinese is not interested in the late night Chinatown trade and compared with Mr Kong (see page 98) and the New Diamond (see page 100) shuts at a positively demurely, positively provincial 11pm during the week, and only half an hour later on the weekends. So it's no good, for after the pub or a club or even, unless you really motor, after the theatre or a concert. Go there instead for lunch and for their dim sum – Shanghai pork buns, BBQ pork pastry, steamed scallop dumplings followed with sweet custard buns, lychee snowballs or sweet bean curd

"Go there instead for lunch and for their dim sum"

pudding. While not up to Royal China (see page 122) or Yauatcha (see page 162), it's perhaps the best dim sum in Chinatown and at the same, especially when they have their half-price weekday lunchtime deal on, some of the cheapest.

118–120 Shaftesbury Avenue, Soho, W1D 5EP
Tel: 020 7437 3077   www.chineseexperience.com   £27
Open: noon–11pm (11.30pm Fri/Sat). Closed Sundays.

Chinese Restaurant 1997

Frugal feasting/Late night

No need to tell you when this Soho Chinese first opened for business, a particularly good year for London restaurants it would seem, with Nobu (see page 101) and Momo (see page 96) also opening. Over a decade later and perhaps it's not held up as well as its famous classmates but Cantonese pop still tinkles from the jukebox and the portraits of Karl Marx and Chairman Mao are still on the walls. The menu is still packed with simple Cantonese staples. It's also still open until the wee hours and has service that's a lot friendlier and more accommodating than much of that on offer over in

"great for after service with the team" – Jonas Karlsson

Chinatown. Jonas Karlsson, executive chef of Harvey Nicks Fifth Floor, does a bit of post work bonding with his kitchen crew there and declares it, "great for after service with the team". Bet it is.

19 Wardour Street, Soho, W1D 6PL
Tel: 020 7734 2868   £17
Open: daily, 5am–4am

Cipriani

Italian

People watch/When someone else pays

The success of this branch of a once exclusive institution, turned unreassuringly expensive international brand, is hard to fathom for some. The marble-tiled interior, all kitsch porthole windows and oversized murals, is not without its charms. But the Italian food is of the comforting but unexceptional variety and scandalously overpriced to boot. Then that's not the point of the Cipriani. Its core clientele of socialites, fashion-types and assorted celebs are rich enough not to have to worry about the inflated price of the starters or the excruciatingly expensive mineral water. They're also, a smattering of suited business types aside, not really that interested in eating.

After dinner here "you'll cancel that appointment with the plastic surgeon" – Fay Maschler

Rather they come to graze, gossip, make merry or show off their latest batch of cosmetic work. As Fay Maschler, *The Evening Standard*'s restaurant critic, notes, after dinner here "You'll cancel that appointment with the plastic surgeon."

25 Davies Street, Mayfair, W1K 3DQ
Tel: 020 7399 0500 www.cipriani.com   £76
Open: daily, noon–2.45pm, 6–11.45pm (10.30pm Sun)

Club Gascon

Abuse the wine list/Dine solo

Long before L'Atelier (see page 23) arrived in London, this Smithfield mainstay was serving small plates inspired by the south-west of France, washed down by wines from the region. A decade later and it's spawned a small empire, comprising the below stairs wine bar Cellar Gascon, the nearby Comptoir Gascon (see page 54) and Le Cercle over by Sloane Square. The shtick is to order three or four starter-size portions from a menu di-

"The focus of the all-French wine list is, like the cooking, the South-West of France."

vided into groups by main ingredient with, this being a Gascony-inspired affair, foie gras famously getting its own section. It can get pricey with the bijou bites running from £12–20-something. An affordable alternative at lunch is the 'Dejeuner Club' menu, which offers three-courses for £28. The focus of the all-French wine list is, like the cooking, the south-west of France from big name Bordeaux to lesser-known producers.

57 West Smithfield, Clerkenwell, EC1A 9DS
Tel: 020 7796 060 www.clubgascon.com
Open: noon–2pm, 7–10pm (10.30pm Fri/Sat). Closed
Sat/Sun lunch.

£62

Comptoir Gascon

French

On-the-hoof

An easy to like delicatessen-cum-bistro that's an infinitely more affordable way to grab a taste of the south-west of France than the nearby Club Gascon (see page 53). It's a dark and meaty destination – and, yes, that's meant as a compliment – where exposed brickwork meets dark wooden floors and the main decoration is the artisan produce on display. Originally more of a deli and less of a bistro, the food and wine sales now serve as an added

extra to the laid back dining. Pork-lovers will be in their ele-

"affordable way to grab a taste of the South West of France"

ment, as there are bits of pig everywhere on the menu, including the perennially popular starter 'Piggy Treats' – ham, fat, ear and two types of sausage. The take-away deli sells everything from freshly baked bread and patisserie to foie gras and wine.

63 Charterhouse Street, Clerkenwell, EC1M 6HJ
Tel: 020 7608 0851 www.comptoirgascon.com   £36
Open: noon–2pm, 7–10pm (11pm Fri/Sat). Deli open
9am–11pm. Both closed Sun/Mon.

Costas Fish Restaurant Fish & chips

Quintessential London

Greek-Cypriot run establishment that, despite the recent luxurious upgrade to its close neighbour and fellow fish 'n' chippery, Geale's, pleasingly shows no sign of changing soon. You walk past the take-away counter and straight through the spotlessly clean kitchen, where Costas himself is usually standing, to the rather nondescript dining room at the back. Weather permitting plump yourself instead at one of the pavement tables.

"the house wine is cheap and drinkable. But let's face it, you're here for the battered fish"

Starters include generous portions of Greek salad, *taramasalata* and *calamari,* and the house wine is cheap and drinkable. But let's face it, you're here for the battered fish, with a choice of cod, plaice, haddock, rock salmon and scampi, served, of course, with chips, and mushy peas, should you desire. You can then return to Greece for a strong coffee and *baklava* to finish, assuming you're not in the market for pineapple or banana fritters.

18 Highgate Street, Notting Hill, W8 7SR
Tel: 020 7727 4310
Open: noon–2.30pm, 5.30–10.30pm Tues–Sat

£10

The Cow   Modern British

Lazy Sunday/Pub grub

It's hard not to fall for the charms of The Cow – Tom Conran's Notting Hill boozer built on a loyal band of boozers, the loyalist of whom stand outside and sneer across at those drinking at the Westbourne opposite. Opened back in 1995 and still in good shape, The Cow is set up like a classic Irish pub, cosy and cramped, with oysters, Guinness and Albanians behind the bar. To Fay

"proof of Conran's Irish extraction"
– Fay Maschler

Maschler, restaurant critic of *The Evening Standard,* it provides, "proof of Conran's Irish extraction". The small downstairs dining room, served by a tiny open kitchen, has a daily changing menu of specials and serves pub staples such as sausage and mash. Upstairs the more formal and pricier Cow dining room is a very civilised place to wile away a Sunday lunch, away from the row below.

89 Westbourne Park Road, Notting Hill, W2 5QH
Tel: 020 7221 0021 www.thecowlondon.co.uk   £33
Open: daily, noon–11pm (10.30pm Sun)

Crazy Homies

Mexican

Dine solo/On-the-hoof

Hipster beards, tasteful tattoos and dressed head-to-toe in American Apparel – but enough about the staff. This packed evening-only noisy Notting Hill Mexican-styled annexe to Lucky 7 (see page 90) is painfully popular with American bankers who, whatever their faults, know their tequilas and tortillas. The ground floor is atmospheric or claustrophobic – depending on whether you have personal space issues – and it fills up early. The

"there's no faulting the cocktails or the well-put-together menu of gentrified Mexican staples"

more spacious basement (famously a former West Indian she-been where in the 60s Christine 'Profumo Affair' Keeler got down and dirty with Stephen Ward and Lucky Gordon) is supposedly open most evenings from 7pm – the whims of the management notwithstanding. But there's no faulting the cocktails or the well-put-together menu of gentrified Mexican staples – *quesadillas*, *tacos*, *burros*, *enchiladas* etc – made with quality ingredients – except perhaps that they don't come cheap.

125 Westbourne Park Road, Notting Hill, W2 5QL
Tel: 020 7727 6771 www.crazyhomieslondon.co.uk   £36
Open: daily, 6pm (noon Sat/Sun)–11pm (10.30pm Sun)

Defune

Japanese

Dine solo/When someone else pays

No one comes to Defune for the ambience and it's unlikely that you will run into any supermodels, actors, footballers, pop stars or celebrities of any description. Add to that an interior that's not terribly glamourous – if anything it's a bit ho-hum. So what does this longstanding Marylebone Japanese share with starry Nobu? If

you're not careful when you're ordering, it can get cripplingly expensive. If that's a

"some of the best authentic Japanese food on offer anywhere in London"

worry, steer for the set menus. With a loyal Japanese staff and clientele, Defune produces some of the best authentic Japanese food on offer anywhere in London. Avoid the downstairs dining room at all costs, particularly if you're prone to depression. The ground-floor sushi bar is where it's at, and where both Giles Coren and restaurateur Alan Yau enjoy taking in the skill of the chefs silently at work, slicing fish for *sashimi* and carefully assembling various sushi rolls.

34 George Street, Marylebone, W1U 7DT
Tel: 020 7935 8311
Open: daily, noon–2.30, 6–10.30pm

£58

Dehesa

Abuse the wine list/Dine solo/Lazy Sunday

This Soho newcomer, from the team behind the similarly setup Saltyard on Goodge Street, does Italian meet Spanish tapas. Once past the chic black awning, the first thing that hits you are the haunches of ham on display around a curved wooden bench. Stools are arranged around a series of high benches and the menu makes the most of its charcuterie before moving on to a selection of small plates such as deep-fried courgette flowers filled with cheese and drizzled with honey; and slow-cooked pork belly with fat cannellini beans. The wine list impresses by weaving its way around lesser known Spanish and Italian regions and grapes. The weekend brunch menu does Spanish and Italian

"The wine list impresses by weaving its way around lesser known Spanish and Italian regions"

things with eggs, such as scramble ducks eggs and serve them with *morcilla* blood sausage and toasted sourdough, and they make a mean Bloody Mary.

25 Ganton Street, Soho, W1F 9BP
Tel: 020 7494 4170 www.dehesa.co.uk   £34
Open: daily, noon (11am Sat/Sun)–11pm (5pm Sun)

Dinings Modern Japanese

Clandestine rendezvous/Dine solo/On-the-hoof

This small but close to perfectly formed modern Japanese bunker is artfully tucked away halfway down a dead-end Marylebone street. Accordingly it's not the sort of place that you just stumble across, so the fact that it's often so busy speaks both of the quality of the food and the building's bijou dimensions. The ground floor sushi bar is pocket-sized while the basement is a series of cosy concrete alcoves – if utilitarian concrete can ever

be considered cosy. Sushi, *sashimi* and a good selection of

> *"Take away orders are put together with as much care and attention to detail as the eat-in" – Terry Durack*

cooked dishes fill out a menu that is bolstered by a blackboard of daily specials from a kitchen overseen by chef/owner Tomonari Chiba (ex of Nobu). "Take away orders are put together with as much care and attention to detail as the eat-in," says Terry Durack, restaurant critic, *Independent on Sunday*, "which is saying something."

22 Harcourt St, Mayfair, W1H 4HH
Tel: 020 7723 0666 £37
Open: noon–2.30pm, 6–10.30pm. Closed Sat lunch and Sun.

Donzoko

Dine solo

Jolly Japanese that's a fairly authentic recreation of what's known in Japan as an *izakaya*, taverns where salarymen drink after work offering food as a means to soak up the sake. From the lantern hung outside to the huge selection of sake and the cramped counter and dining room, everything about Donzoko rings true. The best – and best value – way into the vast menu is perhaps to stick with one of the many set menus. The excellent *yakitori* selection is only available in the evenings,

"the sushi, sashimi, tempura and cooked dishes on offer will still leave you spoilt for choice" but the sushi, *sashimi, tempura* and cooked dishes on offer will still leave you spoilt for choice during the day. You might think the waitresses haven't understood your order but they never seem to make a mistake, and the lady who runs the show might look a little stern but really she has a lovely smile.

15 Kingly Street, Soho, W1B 5PS
Tel: 020 7734 1974   £32
Open: noon–2.30pm, 6–10pm. Closed Sat lunch and Sun.

The Eagle   Mediterranean

Pub grub

The place the unpleasant portmanteau word 'gastropub' was coined to describe, The Eagle is still going about its business very much as it did when it opened back in 1991. Founded by Mike Belben and chef David Eyre, The Eagle was – and is – about hearty helpings of Mediterranean-inspired grub made with seasonal ingredients – think sausages and lentils, grilled swordfish and

peppers. The kitchen sits open, the furniture is mismatched and shabby, as is the

"hearty helpings of Mediterranean-inspired grub"

crockery, and the staff can look at you like they're doing you a favour. It's currently a popular watering hole for hacks from *The Guardian* and *Observer* and always has been, as their offices are just down the road, but don't worry, they're all off to a new building in King's Cross soon. Which will perhaps, at last, make it easier to get a table on a weekday evening.

159 Farringdon Road, Farringdon, EC1R 3AL
Tel: 020 7837 1353   £28
Open: daily, noon–11pm

The East Room

Abuse the wine list

The latest opening from the group behind Milk and Honey, The Player and The Clubhouse, The East Room is a bar, restaurant and member's club, housed in a stylish Victorian Shoreditch conversion. A forward thinking wine bore's wet dream, The East Room bills itself as a 'new world wine room', with a comprehensive list that covers Argentina, Australia, Chile, New Zealand and South Africa. Glasses can be self-served from the help-yourself, every so handy, Italian-made, Enomatic wine dispenser, with over 50 top New World wines available by the glass. It's an interesting attempt to demystify wine. While the roof

"A forward thinking wine bore's wet dream"

terrace and bar are members-only, the dining room is open to the public with a reservation. There, there's likewise a self-service element, with a buffet lunch and dinner always available, as well as a menu that focuses on shared plates.

2a Tabernacle Street, Shoreditch, EC2A 4LU
Tel: 020 7374 9570 www.thstrm.com   £35
Open: 11am (7pm Sat)–1am (3am Thurs–Sat). Closed Sundays.

The Electric Brasserie

French

Breakfast/Dine Solo/Lazy Sunday/People watch/Wish they'd thought of it

You've got to hand it to Soho House supremo Nick Jones – the man knows how to create a scene. The Electric – the collective abbreviation for the brasserie, cinema and members club – changed Portobello Road forever when it opened back in 2002. Still a scene, from breakfast until late at night, it's the former that shows the Electric and Portobello Road – especially when the market is swinging – at its best. Sure it's noisy and the tables are too close together and everybody seems to

shout – but that's partly the point. Eat down the back if you want a civilised chat. Alternatively

"Sure it's noisy and the tables are too close together and everybody seems to shout – but that's partly the point"

take a seat at the zinc-topped bar for a restorative Bloody Mary and eat there, the full breakfast menu – Benedicts, bacon sandwichs, scrambled eggs etc – is available, you get served quicker, and watch the show out front unfold.

191 Portobello Road, Notting Hill, W11 2ED
Tel: 020 7908 9696 www.electricbrasserie.com   £41
Open: 8am (10am Sun)–12.15am (2am Fri/Sat, 11pm Sun)

Faulkner's

Fish & chips

Quintessential London

Mr Faulkner is long gone but this smart East End chippie, which has changed hands several times since, is still the business. That it's a costlier experience than it once was is everything to do with the price of fish. Located on a particularly unpicturesque stretch of Kingsland Road, it's a treat for those prone to seaside nostalgia, with purple shutters on the windows, seafaring pictures on the dark wooden-clad walls and the unmistakable whiff of malt vinegar meeting piping hot starch in the air. The fish, bought every morning from Billingsgate market, is a tried and tested selection that runs alphabetically from cod to skate and is available battered or – for those worried about harden-

"a treat for those prone to seaside nostalgia"

ing arteries – grilled or coated in *matzo* meal. A decidedly less healthy and highly recommended option is their sticky toffee pudding for afters.

424–426 Kingsland Road, Dalston, E8 4AA
Tel: 020 7254 6152   £24
Open: noon–2.30pm, 5 (4.30pm Fri)–10pm Mon–Fri;
11.30am–10pm Sat; noon–9pm Sun

Food Lab

Italian

Breakfast/Dine solo/Frugal feasting

Italian-run Islington café-cum-deli, open for breakfast, lunch and afternoon coffee and cakes. Proprietor Liliana Tamberi is an exuberant Tuscan type who has worked for Giorgio Locatelli and was previously the head chef of Matilda in Battersea. The day starts with sultana scones or bacon and egg stuffed muffins, while lunch options include risotto, salads, pasta and *bruschetta*. It's unlicensed but there are healthy smoothies on offer that are (irritatingly or endearingly – you choose) called things like Love, Sex, Happiness and Recovery. Cakes come courtesy of Nutella tarts and the like. Come the summer there are wicker chairs and an ice-cream cart on the

pavement. It's favourite of food writer and restaurant critic

Great Italian cakes and coffee...and a sweet Italian guy behind the counter" – Caroline Stacey

Caroline Stacey, who says it serves "Great Italian cakes and coffee, has fancy furniture out on the street and a sweet Italian guy behind the counter."

56 Essex Road, Islington, N1 8LR
Tel: 020 7226 1001 www.moodforfood.co.uk   £17
Open: daily, 7am (10am Sun)–5pm (7pm Sat, 4pm Sun)

The Fox & Anchor

Breakfast/Pub grub

Once the favoured boozer of traders from the nearby Smithfield market, it closed, ostensibly for good, back in 2006 – the meat men's early morning breakfasts and beers not enough to keep it in business. Bought by Malmaision, they of the boutique hotel brand, the pub's Victorian interior was recently restored and half a dozen luxury rooms opened above. Although whoever came up with their 'Hops & Chops, Cuvees & Duvets' catchphrase should be given a good slap, the result is that the original bar is now pewter topped and the mahogany and brass fittings have regained their lustre. There are real ales on offer alongside cocktails, champagne and claret for the City

"solid reconstructed pub grub... and you can still get a beer with your breakfast"

boys. Jonas Karlsson, of 5th Floor at Harvey Nichols, welcomes the new kitchen, which does solid reconstructed pub grub, from split pea and ham soup to steak and oyster pie, and you can still get a beer with your breakfast.

115 Charterhouse Street, Clerkenwell, EC1 6AA
Tel: 020 7250 1300 www.foxandanchor.com   £32
Open: daily, 8am (noon Sat/Sun)–11pm (6pm Sun)

Galvin at Windows   Modern French

Breakfast/Clandestine rendezvous/Make an impression/Quintessential London

The wraparound view of London from the 28th floor of the Park Lane Hilton is hard to beat and on a clear day you can see, well, if not forever, at least everything from Buckingham Palace to the West End, making it, for Jay Rayner, the quintessential London experience. The makeover of the restaurant at the summit of this 60s-built landmark was a long time coming. Gone are the buffet and entertainment stage, replaced by lots of cream, dark wood and sets of string curtains. Shame the bar has lost its louche charm in the process. Overseen

by the brothers Galvin, whose Marylebone

"The wraparound view of London from the 28th floor... is hard to beat"

bistrot (see opposite) offers a less elevated experience, the accomplished modern French cooking from Andre Garrett provides more than a distraction from the view. It's a view that's available for breakfast, lunch and dinner and, as you'd expect, doesn't comes cheap.

Park Lane Hilton, 22 Park Lane, Mayfair, W1K 1BE
Tel: 020 7208 4021 www.galvinatwindows.com   £42
Open: 7–10am (10.30am Sat/Sun), noon–3pm, 5.30 (5pm Sat)–11pm. Closed Mon breakfast, Sat lunch and Sun dinner

Galvin Bistrot de Luxe

Abuse the wine list

This simple bistrot from the Galvin brothers, chefs Chris and Jeff, opened in September 2005, helped London fall in love all over again with bourgeois French cooking. An ostensibly unpromising Baker Street site, it was an immediate hit with critics and punters alike for well-priced, educated cooking that made use of best seasonal ingredients, many shipped from Paris' Rungis market. We're talking poached snails, Landaise chicken, duck confit, roast veal brains, *pot au chocolat* – that sort of thing. The

"well-priced, educated cooking that made use of best seasonal ingredients, many shipped from Paris' Rungis market"

wine list again focuses on France with a good number of bottles priced under £30. Down in the basement is the recently opened Le Bar, which has its own menu with oysters, steak tartare, *gnocchi* and the like on offer. Service can be flustered at times but the ooh-la-la-styled dining room, reminiscent of Racine (see page 115), is a pleasure.

66 Baker Street, Marylebone, W1U 7DH

Tel: 020 7935 4007 www.galvinrestaurants.com   £39
Open: noon–2.30pm, 6–10.45pm Mon–Sat; noon–9.30pm Sun

The Garrison

Modern European

Breakfast/Pub grub

What was once the homey Honest Cabbage was reborn several years ago as this light and airy modern pub that evidently suits the good burghers of Bermondsey better. That this is no spit 'n' sawdust boozer is perhaps best illustrated by the fact that it's perhaps the only pub on the planet with a basement cinema that's rented out for private screenings. There's good beer behind the bar and a very reasonably priced wine list. The cooking, that takes from all over Europe, is occasionally a bit too frou frou for its own good, truffle oil where

"perhaps the only pub on the planet with a basement cinema"

it isn't needed and chorizo in the mash. But they do a fine steak sandwich and cheeky bar snacks of cheese on toast and fish finger sarnies. The breakfast menu covers all the bases from Greek yoghurt with fruit salad to the full fry-up.

99–101 Bermondsey Street, Bermondsey, SE1 3XB
Tel: 020 7089 9355 www.thegarrison.co.uk   **£30**
Open: 8am (9am Sat)–11pm Mon–Sat; 9am–10.30pm Sun

Le Gavroche

Abuse the wine list/Be pampered/Make an impression/When someone else pays

Now in its fifth decade, having passed its 40th in style, Le Gavroche has occupied its current Upper Brook Street premises since 1981. Chef Michel Roux Jr has updated the classic haute French cooking of his uncle and

"if they aren't impressed, ditch them" – Fay Maschler

his father, while paying tribute to it, since he took over in a 1991. Dishes, such as lobster mousse with caviar and champagne sauce, are lighter than they would have been a generation ago but remain luxuriant. You no longer need to wear a tie but a jacket is always required. The service, forged under the direction of Silvano Giraldi, who recently retired after 37 years, is spectacularly smooth. Of course it's expensive but the £48 set lunch is exceptionally good value. As Fay Maschler, restaurant critic of *The Evening Standard*, says about anyone you take there, "If they aren't impressed, ditch them."

43 Upper Brook Street, Mayfair, W1K 7QR
Tel: 020 7499 1826 www.le-gavroche.co.uk   £91
Open: noon–2pm, 6.30–11pm. Closed Sat lunch and Sun.

Map

C

Great Queen Street   Modern British

Quintessential London

From the team behind the highly rated Anchor & Hope
(see page 14) Great Queen Street takes the same
approach – affordable gutsy cooking that celebrates
British produce, laid back but friendly service and an intelligent, well-
priced wine list –
to the West End.
Fay Maschler of
*The Evening Stan-
dard* finds it in
possession of "a
singular energy
and total lack of
pretension" that's
uniquely London.
Located opposite
Holborn's impos-
ing Masonic tem-
ple, the look is fa-
miliar; walls paint-
ed bordello red,
floorboards ex-
posed and bare
battered tables. A
long thin room,

*"a singular energy and total lack
of pretension" – Fay Maschler*

with a small downstairs drinking den, it feels – despite a
similarly attractively scruffy staff and surroundings –
more restaurant-like and less pub than the Anchor &
Hope. Taking bookings has brought it to the attention of
many who didn't fancy turning up and taking a punt for
a table at its no-reservations predecessor.

32 Great Queen Street, Holborn, WC2B 5AA

Tel: 020 7242 0622   £32
Open: noon–2.30pm (3pm Sun), 6–10.30pm. Closed Sunday
dinner and Monday lunch.

The Greenhouse

Abuse the wine list/Be pampered/Make an impression/Quintessential London/When someone else pays/Wish they'd thought of it

Marlon Abela, the man from MARC, who also owns UMU (see page 152) and Morton's to name but two, re-launched this famous fine diner in 2004. When former head chef Bjorn van der Hurst defected to Gordon Ramsay, back in it early 2006, it looked bad. But under Executive chef Antonin Bonnet the restaurant has thrived. Some of the best service in London, a discreet, luxurious setting at the end of a pretty Mayfair mews and a

"a wine list that's quite a piece of work"

wine list that's quite a piece of work. "Let them lose on it," suggests Fay Maschler, restaurant critic of The Evening Standard, should someone else be treating you. Then there's Bonnet's assured cooking which takes in Asian influences in dishes such as violet sea urchin, fresh Cornish crab and kombu jelly and keeps it classic with a shared dish of Dover sole meunière.

27a Hay's Mews, Mayfair, W1J 5NY
Tel: 020 7499 3331 www.greenhouserestaurant.co.uk **£86**
Open: noon–2.30pm, 6.45–11pm. Closed Sat lunch and Sun.

Green's

Seafood

Clandestine rendezvous

You can almost smell the mahogany panelling and racing green leather upholstery at this St James' establishment that's proudly Establishment. Sure, most of the 'discerning clientele' are bufferish gents who left their youth behind them – long ago in a land far away – but for many that only adds to its clubbable charms. Within one of its banquetted booths, feels Patrick Williams chef-proprietor of The Terrace, is the perfect place to have a discreet dinner discussion. Presided over by likeable toff restaurateur Simon Parker Bowles, who

"the classic fish-focused menu has been out of fashion for so long that parts of it feel very now"

opened it in 1982, the classic fish focused menu has been out of fashion for so long that parts of it, jellied ham hock, potted shrimp and grilled Dover sole, feel very now. Service is of the old school, to suit the setting, and the wine list is, in places, surprisingly affordable.

36 Duke Street, Mayfair, SW1Y 6DF
Tel: 020 7930 4566 www.greens.org.uk   £51
Open: 11.30am–3pm, 5.30–11pm. Closed Sundays.

Hakkasan

Modern Cantonese

Make an impression/People watch/Wish they'd thought of it

Hakkasan has aged well since it opened back in 2001; it's still a glamour destination and you'll need to enlist the services of a reservation scalper to secure a Friday or Saturday night table at short notice. Famously built on the site of a former underground car park at the end

> "Especially for out-of-towners, it never fails to elicit an oooooh..."
> – Marina O'Loughlin

of a scruffy West End back alley, the space was transformed through restaurateur Alan Yau's vision and Christian Liagre's sultry design, which makes clever use of carved Chinese screens. As *Metro*'s restaurant critic Marina O'Loughlin puts it, "Especially for out-of-towners, it never fails to elicit an oooooh..." But there's substance as well as style to Hakkasan, fine cocktails, a surprisingly good global wine list and modern Cantonese cooking, from chef Tong Chee Hwee, that for many is not just the best in London but some of the best in the world.

8 Hanway Place, Bloomsbury, W1T 1HD
Tel: 0870 141 6099   www.hakkasan.com   £68
Open: noon–3pm (5pm Sat/Sun), 6pm–midnight (11pm Sun)

Hereford Road

British

Abuse the wine list/Lazy Sunday

From the school of St. John (see page 133) this new arrival has brought a gutsy no-nonsense style of cooking, built around British seasonal ingredients, to Notting Hill.

Driven by hard-working chef proprietor Tom Pemberton, formerly head chef of St John Bread & Wine (see page 134), who seems to be permanently standing behind the stove, Hereford Road is housed in what was once a Victorian butchers and more recently saw action as Veronica's. The loveseats facing the kitchen at the front of the restaurant, where the ceiling is decorated with wrought metal, are perfect

"gutsy no-nonsense style of cooking, built around British seasonal ingredients"

for two. The dining room down the back is perhaps rather too austere but brightened by the pleasant service. But it's the well-priced wine list and menu, which delivers everything from a whole fish to huge helpings of oxtail or a perfect lemon sorbet, that's the real draw.

3 Hereford Road, Notting Hill, W2 4AB
Tel: 020 7727 1144 www.herefordroad.org   £38
Open: daily, noon–3pm, 6–10.30pm (10pm Sun)

Hibiscus

Make an impression

A recent arrival in Mayfair, transplanted from Ludlow in Shropshire, where this husband and wife run operation won awards and generous critical praise for over seven years, Hibiscus has, after a difficult start, hit the ground running. The cutting edge French cooking from Lyon-

"cutting edge French cooking from Lyon-born chef Claude Bosi"

born chef Claude Bosi fills the restaurant, while his wife Claire oversees the front of house with a keen young staff, many of whom also made the journey down from Ludlow. An intimate wood-panelled dining room with the kitchen discreetly tucked away at the back, it's a lot less stuffy than that sounds. The cooking in complex combinations such as Limousin veal kidney – cooked in duck fat, confit of vine tomatoes in muscovado sugar, globe artichoke puree, brown shrimp cream – makes sure of that. Eating from the set lunch menu is an affordable way to enjoy this haute experience.

29 Maddox Street, Mayfair, W1S 2PA
Tel: 020 7629 2999 www.hibiscusrestaurant.co.uk   £87
Open: noon–2.30pm, 6.30–10pm. Closed Sat/Sun.

Hix Oyster & Chophouse   British

Lazy Sunday/People watch/Quintessential London/Wish they'd thought of it

After years overseeing the menus for Caprice Holdings' famous stable of restaurants and successfully relaunching Scott's (see p126) the chef director and Bill Murray doppelganger, Mark Hix, decided to depart for fresh pastures in 2007. After helping out over at the Albemarle

(see page 13) he opened this his first eponymous joint on what was previously the site of the old fish restaurant, Rudland & Stubbs. The menu is trademark Hix, reviving and reinventing classic and forgotten British delicacies such as skate knobs, smoking his own salmon and serving uncommon cuts such as sirloin on the bone. Hix's thirsty crew of arty cronies have followed him over from the Rivington Grill in Shoreditch (which he sold to his former employers before he did one) and is supplemented by a steady supply of restaurant industry types. The service can be a shambles.

"reviving and reinventing classic and forgotten British delicacies"

36–37 Greenhill Rents, Cowcross Street, Clerkenwell, EC1M 6BN
Tel: 020 7017 1930 www.restaurantsetcltd.co.uk   £47
Open: noon–3pm, 6–11pm. Closed Saturday lunch and Sunday dinner.

Hung Tao

Frugal feasting

Betwixt the tourist tat of Queensway, just down from royally posher Royal China (see page 122), this small cheery Chinese is a favourite haunt of food hack Tom Parker Bowles, who finds it "stupidly cheap with fine *congee* and noodle soups". The sustaining one-bowl meals that come via the aforementioned noodle soups and more solid stuff, such as duck rice, are a draw for everyone from underfunded students, to slumming-it scribes for *The Mail on Sunday*. The décor's not much to look at, the dining room sparsely decked out in substandard Chinatown chic, while the service gets the food from the kitchen to the table – sometimes

"stupidly cheap with fine congee and noodle soups"
— Tom Parker Bowles

with a smile. But forget it's the superbly barbecued meats (*char sui*, crispy pork, chicken and duckling) on display in the window that, unless you're a vegetarian, you should be focusing on.

51 Queensway, Bayswater, W2 4QH
Tel: 020 7727 5753
Open: daily, 11am–11pm

£12

Indian Zing   Modern Indian

Make an impression/Worth the schlep

On an ordinary looking parade of shops in an unremarkable section of suburban west London, chef-proprietor Manoj Vasaikar's (ex of Chutney Mary and Veeraswamy) Indian Zing produces some of the best modern Indian cooking in London. While the menu takes in much of the sub-continent and adds modish touches with Zing's Shikampuri kebab (minced chicken stuffed with asparagus and cottage cheese), Vasaikar is Mumbai-born and so the emphasis often falls on south Indian flavours. The spicing, in starters such as *patrani macchi* (a fillet of a suitably seasonal fish marinated in green herbs and coconut and steamed in banana leaves) and main

"some of the best modern Indian cooking in London"

courses of Karwari fish curry, is superb. Desserts throw in a bit of fusion with a *masala* bread and butter pudding. The interior is surprisingly plush, with a covered terrace at the back, while service veers towards the charmingly formal.

236 King Street, Hammersmith, W6 0RF
Tel: 020 8748 5959 www.indianzing.co.uk   £33
Open: noon (1pm)–3pm, 6–11pm (11.30pm Sat, 10pm Sun)

J Sheekey

Dine solo/Make an impression/People watch

Lesser celebrated than its starry stable-mates, The Ivy and Le Caprice, J Sheekey has been serving fish, bar a few breaks for World Wars and refurbishments, since the late 19th century. Smack bang in the centre of Theatreland, but cut off from its hubbub in a quiet courtyard, its regulars don't care that Scott's, which specialises in a

similarly polished approach to seafood, has since been revamped. Particularly as most of the dishes on the menu there were here first. Both Mark Hix and Angela Hartnett believe eating at the bar alone is a pleasurable experience, with the clientele worth a gander, especially Giles Coren trying to make an impression on his guests in the cor-

"a new 30-seat oyster bar to serve waifs and strays without bookings"

ner. The service is polished throughout a series of dining alcoves decked out in leather and wood. It can be a pricey experience but the three-course weekend lunch menu at £24.75 isn't. They've recently opened a new 30-seat oyster bar to serve waifs and strays without bookings.

28–32 St Martin's Court, Covent Garden, WC2N 4AL
Tel: 020 7240 2565 www.caprice-holdings.co.uk   **£52**
Open: daily, noon–3pm (3.30pm Sun), 5.30pm (6pm Sun)
–midnight (11pm Sun)

Japan Centre (Toku) Japanese/Sushi

Dine solo/Frugal feasting

Housed on the ground floor of the Japan Centre on Piccadilly, a treasure trove of all things Japanese from general groceries and one of the best off-sale sake selections in town, to various books and knick-knacks, Toku serves simple authentically good Japanese food. The sushi, the rice for which is cooked over bamboo charcoal, and *sashimi* is good enough for Ichiro Kubota, head chef of Umu (see page 152), and many other homesick Japanese, to invest in when grabbing a budget bite. *Ramen*, *udon* and *soba* noodles and the usual *bento* boxes

and set meals, with free refills of *miso* soup until you just can't take no more,

"good enough for Ichiro Kubota, head chef of Umu, and many other homesick Japanese"

make up the rest of the menu. On the second Tuesday of every month Toku closes in the afternoon to become the JC Sushi Academy, where you can learn to slice and roll your own.

212–213 Piccadilly, Mayfair, W1J 9HX
Tel: 020 7255 8255 www.toku-restaurant.co.uk   £26
Open: daily, noon–10pm (8pm Sun)

Jen Café

Frugal feasting/On-the-hoof

Ramshackle little corner caff on the edge of Chinatown, that's a good vantage point from which to watch the comings and goings around Gerrard Street. Open from noon to early evening it provides satisfying snacks of noodle soup, freshly made dumplings – steamed and griddled, and various barbecued treats in helpings of *char sui*, duck and crispy pork. Frequented by the odd tourist, that's happened upon it en route to Leicester Square or Piccadilly Circus, and gaggles of giggling Chinese girls, who come as it's one of the few place in London that

"provides satisfying snacks of noodle soup, freshly made dumplings ... and various barbecued treats"

serves a large selection of bubble drinks, from watermelon to milky Taiwanese green tea, iced and made with pearls of chewable tapioca, that are sucked up with wide straws and then gently gnawed. An acquired taste but worth a try especially as it's unlicensed. Service is smiley but chaotic.

4–8 Newport Place, Soho, WC2H 7JP
Tel: 020 7287 9708   £18
Open: daily, noon–8pm (8.30pm Sat/Sun)

Joe Allen

American

Breakfast/Late night/Lazy Sunday/People watch

It's air-kissing luvvies a go-go at this Covent Garden thespian favourite since 1977. While it could be argued that some of the theatrical types who make up the clientele are prone to pretension, the same cannot be said of the easy-going US menu that always finds room for Caesar salad, pork chops and pecan pie – although not for the famous 'secret' burger. The à la carte prices aren't for struggling actors but the weekday lunch and weekend brunch menus, the latter including two-courses, a

"Late at night it's still the place"
— *Jay Rayner*

glass of champagne, Bucks Fizz or Bloody Mary for £18.50, are infinitely better value, and a WiFi enabled breakfast is available Monday to Friday. The basement dining room is packed to the exposed bricks most nights and Jay Rayner, the *Observer*'s restaurant critic, who's always wanted to be on stage, says, "Late at night it's still the place."

13 Exeter Street, Covent Garden, WC2E 7DT
Tel: 020 7836 0651 www.joeallen.co.uk   £43
Open: daily, 8am (11.30am Sat/Sun)–12.45am (11.45pm Sun)

Kensington Square Kitchen

Clandestine rendezvous/Dine solo

Daytime-only licensed café from Leith's lady cookery school graduate, overlooking a pleasant garden square behind Kensington High Street. A haven for hassled shoppers, it does a good line in seasonal soups, salads, small plates and more substantial meals, in the way of good quality burgers, pasta and pies – with freshly baked cakes for afters. The sort of place more common to Sydney or northern California, it's open for breakfast from 9am and starts doing its laid-back brunch thing at midday, with a decent drinks list, staying open until 6pm. Aimed at the glamorous mums who drop their kids off

"aimed at the glamorous mums who drop their kids off at the nearby primary school"

at the nearby primary school, it's prettily decorated, like a posh childless housewife's parlour, scattered with glossy food porn publications. There are additional seats in the basement but on a sunny day you want to be sitting upstairs overlooking the square.

9 Kensington Square, Kensington, W8 5EP　　£24
Tel: 020 7938 2598　www.kensingtonsquarekitchen.co.uk
Open: 8.30am–5pm (5.30 Sat) Mon–Sat; 5.30–10.30pm Tues–Thurs

Kiasu

Straits Malaysian

Frugal feasting/On-the-hoof

The walls of Kiasu are scrawled with things to be afraid of, from getting fat to going mad. Beyond that and the fact that it is trimmed in bright blue and harshly lit the cafeteria-style interior of Kiasu (which is Hokkien Chinese for 'afraid to be second best') is pretty nondescript, evidently built for speed and not comfort but regularly packed with smiling faces. They come for the keenly priced plates on the Straits of Malacca inspired menu that also takes in (although admittedly less successfully) odd bits and pieces of Thai and Vietnamese. According

to Bill Knott (editor-at-large, *Yes Chef!*) it's "The next best thing to grazing in a night market in Singapore or Penang,"

"The next best thing to grazing a night market in Singapore or Penang" – Bill Knott

while food writer Andy Lynes talks of "Generous portions of delicious and authentic Malaysian and Singaporean dishes," and warmly recommends "the superb *roti*".

48 Queensway, Bayswater, W2 3RY
Tel: 020 7727 8810 www.kiasu.co.uk
£29
Open: daily, noon–11pm

Lahore Kebab House

Frugal feasting

This unlicensed East End kebab house has been the bolthole of choice for News International's finest since they moved to nearby Wapping. Once a small, scruffy, unloved-looking joint full of suited hacks with six-packs – of beer that is – its success saw it stay scruffy but expand into neighbouring premises and there's now room enough for close to the whole editorial team of *The Times*, should they all fancy it one lunchtime. No doubt Rupert Murdoch could afford it, particularly as the simple menu of kebabs and curries are as cheap as it gets. Although some can't help but pine for the good old days when the place was about a tenth of the size and it still felt like a secret, the *tikkas* –

"the simple menu of kebabs and curries are as cheap as it gets"

mutton, chicken and *paneer* – are still particularly good, as are the *biryanis*, breads and *dal*.

2 Umberston Street, Whitechapel, E1 1PY
Tel: 020 7488 2551 www.lahorekebabhouse.com   £13
Open: daily, noon–midnight

Locanda Locatelli

Italian

Be pampered/Clandestine rendezvous/Make an impression/People watch

The starriest Italian restaurant in town is, like all the best Italians, not about over-elaborate cooking but simple, produce-focused brilliance and warm hospitality. Driven by the husband and wife team of Giorgio and Plaxy Locatelli, despite a dining room that at times feels like a big budget 1970s porn set, it's one of the most child-friendly upmarket restaurants in London, with a kitchen that's more than happy to cater for even the most obscure food allergies. A celebrity favourite where the paparazzi often lurk outside, the stars come here for the Northern Italian menu that does justice to *antipasti*, pasta, meat, game, fish and *dolci*. The service – depend-

"simple, produce-focused brilliance and warm hospitality"

ing on whether they need the table back or not, with oversubscribed evening slots typically two-hours – can make you feel like a star, or a star in a hell of a hurry.

8 Seymour Street, Marylebone. W1H 7J2
Tel: 020 7935 9088   www.locandalocatelli.com   £55
Open: daily, noon–3pm (3.15pm Sat/Sun), 6.45–11pm
(11.30pm Sat, 10.15pm Sun)

London Capital Club

Breakfast/Clandestine rendezvous

This plush private club in heart of the Square Mile, set in suitably resplendent Grade-II listed premises, is within shouting distance of the Bank of England, Lloyd's and the Stock Exchange. Accordingly it plays host to a paying membership of City executives who use it for business entertaining. Although it's members-only at lunchtime, its restaurants, the Walbrook Grill and the Club Brasserie, can be booked by the great unwashed for dinner and breakfast respectively. The latter, served Monday to Friday, in a handsome modern dining room

"the perfect start to the day for anyone who wants to play at being a captain of industry"

on the lower ground floor that's decked out with ochre leather banquettes, is the perfect start to the day for anyone who wants to play at being a captain of industry. Options run from healthy porridge oats with honey, to the hearty London Capital Club Full English that includes Cumberland sausage and black pudding.

15 Abchurch Lane, City, EC4N 7BW
Tel: 020 7717 0088   www.londoncapitalclub.com   £45
Open: 6–10pm Mon–Fri

Lucky 7

Diner

Breakfast/Dine solo/On-the-hoof

Lucky 7 is a hip miniaturised simulation of a US diner. Its booths are trimmed with green vinyl and mock stone cladding, there's assorted Americana on the walls and a pin-board menu stretching over the open-plan kitchen. It does a fine line in serving up State-side-style break-fasts including two-eggs-any-style (with your choice of pork product), omelettes, butter-milk pancakes and French toast. The attention to detail extends to sourcing such things as sausage patties. They even have bot-tomless cups of drip-fed coffee. After breakfast it's about quality

"a fine line in serving Stateside-style breakfasts, quality burgers and made-to-order milkshakes"

burgers (made with organic Aberdeen Angus) fries (fat or skinny) and made-to-order milkshakes that come in various flavours and thicknesses. Fully licensed with cocktails, bottled beer and wine on offer. Avoid at the weekends when the wait for a late breakfast slot can be particularly trying. Not for those who consider booth-sharing a bitch.

127 Westbourne Park Road, Notting Hill, W2 5QL
Tel: 020 7727 6771   www.lucky7london.co.uk   £38
Open: daily, 10am (9am Sat/Sun)–11pm (10.30pm Sun)

Magdalen

Abuse the wine list/Clandestine rendezvous/Dine solo

Smart two-storey operation run by a talented young trio who have pooled their enviable collective experience from the Anchor & Hope (see page 14), La Trompette (see page 151), The Fat Duck and Le Manoir Aux Quat' Saisons. It's bordello-red walls, simply dressed tables and exposed floorboards throughout. The low-key ground floor, which doesn't take reservations, offers the same seasonal daily changing menu as the more clubbable upstairs dining room. The cooking, which makes use of nearby Borough Market and loves a bit of rare breed, is refined-gutsy in starters the likes of cured sea trout and dill, and fried pig's head. Shared main courses, typically big bits of meat and game, always make an appearance, as

"The cooking makes use of nearby Borough Market"

do simple but accomplished sweet things such as a cherry and almond tart. The service is together and the affordable French-leaning wine list is something Tom Pemberton feels is well worth investigating.

152 Tooley Street, Bermondsey, SE1 2TU
Tel: 020 7403 1342 www.magdalenrestaurant.co.uk   £39
Open: noon–2.30pm, 6.30–10.30pm. Closed Sat lunch, Sun and 2 weeks in August.

Mango & Silk

Indian

Frugal feasting/Lazy Sunday/Worth the schlep

A new home in East Sheen for seasoned Indian chef Udit Sarkhel who came out of retirement – he moved to Brighton and took up painting after shutting Sarkhel's in Southfields – to get behind of the stoves at this small neighbourhood restaurant late in 2007. This is no bog standard suburban tandoori, although it shouldn't surprise you to hear that it's really not worth the journey for the setting alone. Rather take yourself, to what estate agents like to refer to as Mortlake, for Sarkhel's way with an ambitious pan-Indian menu that takes in Parsi, Mughal, Punjabi and south Indian dishes, and makes use of seasonal British bits and pieces where possible. A favourite of William Sitwell,

"an ambitious pan-Indian menu that takes in Parsi, Mughal, Punjabi and south Indian dishes"

the curry loving editor of *Waitrose Food Illustrated*, everything from Hyderabadi chicken sixers to the lamb coconut *bhoona* delivers, as does the finely affordable Sunday lunch buffet.

199 Upper Richmond Road, Mortlake, SW14 8QT
Tel: 020 8876 6220 www.mangoandsilk.co.uk   £21
Open: noon–3pm Sun only, 6–10pm (10.30pm Fri/Sat).
Closed Mondays and 2 weeks in August.

Market

Frugal feasting

This casual Camden diner is a more than welcome addition to an area where it's slim pickings for eating out and more about scabby pubs of the 'doesn't-Amy-Winehouse-show-up-and-act-like-an-anaesthetised-paparazzi-poodle-there?' variety. Aside from chairs that make for a sitting experience that will take you back to the classroom everything else clicks. The exposed brick walls, open kitchen and zinc-topped tables work well together in a dining room that's big on buzz. Prices, including the easy to get along with wine list, are reasonable. There's friendly service and from chef Dan Spence, ex of Exmouth Market's Medcalf, the generous portions (the chicken and ham pie is a beast and

"There's friendly service... and generous portions"

the jam pudding will keep you warm at night) of fuss-free modern British food – of a style that you shouldn't be able to screw up but a lot of restaurants still do – are spot on.

43 Parkway, Camden, NW1 7PN
Tel: 020 7267 9700
Open: noon–2.30pm, 6–10.30pm Mon–Sat; 1–4pm Sun

£32

Maroush I   Belly dancing Lebanese

Late night

This, the first branch of Maroush, opened in 1981 and founded an empire that today includes Randa, Ranoush (see page 116), Beirut Express (see page 28) and Sidi Maaroof and extends along much of the Edgware Road with further outposts in Chelsea, Kensington and Knightsbridge. Although some branches of Maroush ap-

pear to have interchangeable menus, this is still very much the flagship of the group and as such has an especially vast 50-strong *meze* selection and a particularly lengthy meat-heavy list of char-grilled Lebanese specialities, laced with such offal treats as *beid ghanem* (lambs' testicles). Portions are generous to a fault and on a good night the

"somewhere that has live Arabic music and belly dancing every night"

service (erring towards old school formal) can be charm itself. A typically late night affair, it's decked out very much as you'd expect for somewhere that has live Arabic music and belly dancing every night from 9.30pm.

21 Edgware Road, Marylebone, W2 2JE
Tel: 020 7723 0773 www.maroush.com   £43
Open: daily, noon–2am (live acts from 9.30pm)

Maze

Make an impression/When someone else pays

Run by Jason Atherton, the ambitious rising star of Gordon Ramsay Holdings, Maze has its faults. The ostensibly fine setting, overlooking Grosvenor Square, is spoilt by the concrete security barricades outside the American Embassy opposite. Then there's the design of the room – too much veneer, too many unnecessary curves, too bland, too corporate hotel. Let's just call it an acquired taste. Not so Jason Atherton's cooking. The first

"Atherton's cooking... takes in new techniques and applies them to French cooking"

British chef to do time in the kitchen at legendary Spanish destination El Bulli, his CV also includes time under acclaimed haute French purveyors Pierre Koffman and Nico Ladenis. Atherton's cooking, some of London's best, takes in new techniques and applies them to French cooking while never forgetting that he's British in dishes such as Cornish red mullet, sardine and saffron rice with paella air, and Arctic roll with raspberry jelly.

10–13 Grosvenor Square, Mayfair, W1K 6JP
Tel: 020 7495 2211   www.gordonramsay.com   £67
Open: daily, 6.45–10.30am, noon–2.30pm (3.30pm Sat/Sun),
5.45–11pm.

Momo

North African

**Clandestine rendezvous/Make an impression/
People watch**

Mourad Mazouz's little piece of North Africa in the heart
of the West End celebrated its first decade in style not
so long ago. The Mo tearoom is a laid back affair – it has
to be with seating that low. It's good for a drink – the
mint tea is the real poured-from-a-great-height deal or
one of the well-made cocktails, a snack or – assuming
it's not snowing outside since the change in the law – a
go on a shisha pipe. The main restaurant – it shouldn't
surprise you – is a touch more formal. The menu is a

*"the mint tea is the real poured-
from-a-great-height deal"*

mixture of takes
on classic North
African dishes
such as pigeon *pastilla*, various *tagines* and *couscous* combinations; and a handful of more modern combinations
such as veal cutlets with fennel, spinach and wild mush-
rooms. Meanwhile, down in the basement, the Kemia
bar still jumps.

25 Heddon Street, Mayfair, W1B 4BH
Tel: 020 7434 4040   www.momoresto.com   £49
Open: noon–2.30pm, 6.30–11.30pm (11pm Sun). Closed
Sunday lunch.

Mr Jerk (The Original)   Caribbean

Map
C

Frugal feasting/On-the-hoof

Once upon a time there was Soho jerk joint called Mr Jerk, then the two business partners went their separate ways, except they did and they didn't. What was the site of the original Mr Jerk is now called Jerk City and run by one of half the once dynamic Mr Jerk duo, while directly next door on a new site, run by the other partner, lies this, known henceforth as the Original Mr Jerk. Confused? You should be but there's nothing baffling about the menu of comforting West Indian staples that, in addition to the celebrated jerk chicken, includes curry mutton, ox-

"comforting West Indian staples"

tail, brown stew fish, ackee and saltfish and various *roti*. Spacious and luxurious compared to the original Mr Jerk, the Original Mr Jerk is more restaurant less take-away, but still the perfect place for Pat Williams, chef at the Terrace, to eat on the fly, perched at the bar sipping a Sour Sap punch.

187 Wardour Street, Soho, W1F 8ZB
Tel: 020 7437 7770 www.mrjerk.co.uk   £25
Open: 11am–11pm Mon–Sat; noon–8pm Sun

Map C

Mr Kong

Cantonese

Frugal feasting/Late night

Long-running late night Cantonese that's more welcoming than many of its Chinatown competitors by virtue of its charming manager, if not the trademark grumpiness of some of the other staff. It's the after hours choice of

"baked razor clams in the small hours" – Charles Campion

both Fay Maschler, restaurant critic of *The Evening Standard*, who declares it "Even better since the re-fit"; and Charles Campion, editor of *The London Restaurant Guide*, who goes there for "baked razor clams in the small hours". Scruffily decorated, it's spread over three floors; try and bag one of the dozen ground floor tables, where you're likely to get more attention.

The main menu runs through the usual Anglo-Cantonese staples from chicken and sweetcorn soup to sweet and sour pork. But you're better delving into the more off beat specials such as pig's knuckle with jellyfish or baked soft-shell crab with chilli and spicy salt.

21 Lisle Street, Soho, WC2H 7BA
Tel: 020 7437 7341
Open: daily, noon–2am

£27

Nahm

Be pampered/Clandestine rendevous

The best Thai restaurant in London by some way is Australian-powered. The cooking at chef David Thomson's restaurant refines Thai flavours into an haute experience via a complex series of soups, dumplings, curries and stir-fries. But he's no mere gastronomic interloper and, despite the fact that he's a man from Down Under, is one of the world's leading authorities on Thai cooking, even working as a consultant to the Thai government on the subject. Service at Nahm is polite and attentive, in the way classy hotels are, and the wine list is full of bottles to ably match the Thai flavours. Its location in the Halkin hotel in Belgravia, which likes to boast its

"one of the world's leading authorities on Thai cooking, even working as a consultant to the Thai government"

exclusivity, means it's sometimes a bit too exclusive during the day. Which makes it perfect for taking someone special for an expensively discreet long lunch.

The Halkin Hotel, Halkin Street, Belgravia, SW1X 7DJ
Tel: 020 7333 1234 www.nahm.como.bz   £62
Open: noon–2.30pm, 7–11pm (10pm Sun). Closed Sat/Sun lunch.

Map
C

New Diamond

Cantonese

Late night

A Lisle Street late night, after service favourite for many of the Capital's chefs including Jason Atherton of Maze (see page 95) and Mark Edwards of Nobu (see opposite), open until 3am every night. Within an interior that looks early 1980s, but was redone much more recently, a vast Cantonese menu is served. Chefs aside it has loyal followers, including randomly, if you read the cuttings proudly displayed in the window, Mel Brooks. The menu is a mix of workday set menus and a long à la carte containing all your Cantonese favourites. There's a lot more interesting stuff if you can read Chinese or get one of the waiting staff to translate for you. As another chef fan, Jeremy Lee of

"The staff are sweet and the food is good – just don't focus on the interior" – Jeremy Lee

the Blueprint Café, puts it, "The staff are sweet and the food is good – just don't focus on the interior."

23 Lisle Street, Soho, WC2H 7BA
Tel: 020 7437 2517   £21
Open: daily, noon–3am

Nobu

Map

B

Dine solo/People watch/When someone else pays

Although London contains three Nobu restaurants, including the nearby Nobu Berkeley and Ubon near Canary Wharf, this Park Lane branch in the Metropolitan hotel is still the famous flagship and not just because it

was here that Boris Becker entertained a model in the broom cupboard. It's still packed with celebrities who stay out of the storage space but order from the luxurious modern Japanese menu that famously borrows from Peru and beyond. The dining room is unlovably utilitarian but no one seems to notice when they're eating their rock shrimp *tempura* and black cod or sampling the sake. Getting a table at short notice, particularly in the evening, is a battle unless you have an agent or are sleeping with one of the management and then, hopefully, in a rather plush suite upstairs and not just another cupboard.

"The dining room is unlovably utilitarian but no one seems to notice"

Metropolitan Hotel, 19 Old Park Lane, Mayfair, W1
Tel: 020 7447 4747 www.noburestaurants.com   £91
Open: noon–2.15pm, 6–10.15pm Mon–Fri; 12.30–2.30pm, 6–11pm (9.30pm Sun) Sat/Sun

19 Numara Bos Cirrik

Turkish

Frugal feasting/Worth the schlep

The scintillating stretch of the Stoke Newington Road where this lies is the centre of Dalston's Turkish restaurant enclave. 19 Numara Bos Cirrik's neighbours number a branch of the mighty Mangal and Istanbul Isembecisi, once the greatest and still the grandest Turkish restaurant in town and now mostly noteworthy because it's open until 5am. 19 Numera Bos Cirrik shuts up shop a lot a lot earlier, lacks the chandeliers and looks like a small nondescript café but few – and certainly not Charles Campion, of the *London Restaurant Guide* who speaks of its "magnificent grilled meats" –

"Magnificent grilled meats"
– Charles Campion

would deny that it's the current reigning Turk. Cooked on an *ocakbasi* grill the meats – mostly bits of lamb – from spare ribs to kidneys, and pieces of poultry – from chicken to quail – are done to perfection. Vegetarians can chew on a stuffed onion.

34 Stoke Newington Road, Dalston, N16 7XJ
Tel: 020 7249 0400   £21
Open: daily, noon–midnight

Oslo Court

Be pampered/Clandestine rendezvous

Hidden from passing trade on the ground floor of a St John's Wood mansion block, in what was once a drinking den for Norwegian airmen, with a menu that's not changed since the 70s and a colour scheme that would have made the late Barbara Cartland blush – Oslo Court is perhaps the most pleasingly bizarre dining experience

"perhaps the most pleasingly bizarre dining experience in London"

in London. Not that its clientele of genteel Jewish pensioners see anything untoward in the salmon walls, the crisp peachy-pink napery and a menu that comprises an encyclopaedic list of dishes that were last in fashion before Elvis started to bloat. Melba toast, an abundance of brandy and cream sauces, and lots of flambéing and friendly fawning silver service is what you get and what Square Meal's Ben McCormack loves. The camp Egyptian waiter who comes along with the dessert trolley at the end is a memorable closing act.

Prince Albert Road, St John's Wood, NW8 7EN
Tel: 020 7722 8795   £61
Open: 12.30–2.30pm, 7–11pm. Closed Sundays and August.

E Pellicci

Greasy Spoon

Breakfast/Frugal feasting/Quintessential London/Worth the schlep

This East End caff that's been run by the Pellicci family since 1900 with a 1946 interior that's been listed by English National Heritage, is one classy-looking greasy spoon. Back in the 50s there were hundreds of places like this, run by Italian families, and now – partly thanks to Starbucks syndrome – it's one of the last of its kind. Within its veneer-panelled-Formica-table-topped interior, breakfast is served, every day save Sunday, from 6.15am. The lunch options include pies, chops, liver, spag bol, and things that go well with custard such as jam roly-poly, syrup sponge and bread 'n' butter pudding. Full of family-run community spirit, Pellicci hasn't changed since the Krays were regulars. A special place to tuck into a standard fry-up, it's the breakfast venue of choice for Angela Hartnett, Chef of Murano in Mayfair and a Bethnal Green local.

"Pellicci's hasn't changed since the Krays were regulars"

332 Bethnal Green Road, Bethnal Green, E2
Tel: 020 7739 4873
£12
Open: 6.15am–4.45pm. Closed Sundays

Petersham Nurseries Modern Eclectic

A

Worth the schlep

Only still in London in the sense that it's at the end of the Richmond branch of the district line and then still a 10-minute cab ride or a 30-minute stroll away, this day-time-only tea house and restaurant occupies a boho space between the potting sheds in the centre of a posh

"Australian chef Skye Gyngell... likes to make use of British produce at its seasonal peak"

nursery. As well as being a bugger to get to, it's an arse to secure a reservation – probably because the likes of Richard Corrigan, Alan Yau, Angela Hartnett and Mourad Mazouz all agree it's well worth the effort, and, for somewhere that's only does lunch and spot of afternoon tea, has possibly the most compli-cated opening hours ever con-ceived between the tea house and the restaurant. That said, and despite the ambitious pricing, it's consistently considered worth the journey for the unique setting and the cooking, by Australian chef Skye Gyngell, that likes to make use of British produce at its seasonal peak in soups and salads in summer and stews and casseroles come the winter.

Church Lane, Petersham, Surrey, TW10 7AG
Tel: 020 8605 3627 www.petershamnurseries.com   £57
Open: noon–2.45pm. Closed Mondays.

La Petite Maison
French

Abuse the wine list/Be pampered/Clandestine rendevous/Lazy Sunday

A recent side project for Arjun Waney, the cash behind Zuma (see page 163) and Roka (see page 121), La Petite Maison is an offshoot of the old Nice hotspot of the same name. With its luxuriously bourgeois French menu,

"its luxuriously bourgeois French menu... was an instant hit with many, including the critics"

it was an instant hit with many, including the critics who slavered praise over the luxurious whole roast Black Leg chicken stuffed with foie gras. Much of the menu is designed to share, starting with a series of hors d'oeuvres, a now fashionable way to commence since it was brought in at Le Café Anglais (see page 40). Comforting mains include the like of truffled macaroni or salt-baked sea bass, and desserts are classics such as *crème* brûéee and apple tart. The service is suave and smooth (although it takes an hour for that chicken) and the all-French wine list with 16 selections by the glass is also a winner.

54 Brooks Mews, Mayfair, W1K 4EG
Tel: 020 7495 4774   www.lpmlondon.co.uk   £53
Open: noon–2.15pm, 6–10.15pm. Closed Sunday evening.

Pétrus

Abuse the wine list/Be pampered/Clandestine rendezvous/Make an impression/When some-one else pays

By the time you read this Pétrus may no longer exist or it may exist in a location other than Knightsbridge's Berkeley Hotel, still run by Gordon Ramsay Holdings, but without Marcus Wareing, the chef who forged its reputation, who will be elsewhere. Hopefully he'll still be at the Berkeley in the same kitchen with the same dining room, running a restaurant that's most likely to be called Marcus Wareing at the Berkeley. The unseemly squabble

"an haute experience with few equals in London"

between Wareing and former boss Gordon Ramsay hasn't stopped this restaurant, whatever it's now called, from being an haute experience with few equals in London. The service is silky under the equally smooth restaurant manager Jean-Philippe Susilovic, the wine list is immense and Wareing's cooking, in combinations such as pan fried foie gras, rhubarb poached with Lapsang tea, quince and hazelnut, is in its pomp.

The Berkeley, Wilton Place, Knightsbridge, SW1X 7RL
Tel: 020 7592 1609 www.gordonramsay.com/petrus £85
Open: noon–2.30pm, 6–11pm. Closed Sat lunch and Sun.

Pho

Vietnamese

Frugal feasting/On-the-hoof

The original branch of what's now a small chain, this branded Vietnamese café named after the national dish, a comforting spicy rice noodle soup to which various things can be added, was opened by a British couple inspired by a Ho Chi Minh City holiday. Simply furnished in a perfectly acceptable modern cafeteria fashion, Pho demystifies and packages Vietnamese food for those that don't have the time (City workers) or the inclination (suburban scaredy-cats) to take a mosey along Hackney's Kingsland Road to check out the likes of Viet Grill (see page 153) and

"Pho demystifies and packages Vietnamese food for those that don't have the time"

Sông Qué (see page 130). The menu mostly sticks to *pho*, with ten or more varieties such as *pho chin bo vien* (with beef meatballs and brisket) usually available for take away or eating in, *bun* – rice noodles with various toppings, and *banh mi* – Vietnamese baguette sandwiches.

86 St John Street, Clerkenwell, EC1M 4EH
Tel: 020 7253 7624   www.phocafe.co.uk   £18
Open: noon–3pm, 6–10pm Mon–Fri; 6.30–10.30pm Sat

Pied à Terre

Clandestine rendezvous/When someone else pays

A modern haute institution, Pied à Terre is one of a handful of gastronomic London restaurants that's neither attached to a hotel or restaurant group, although that said, they've recently opened a second, more modest Marylebone site called L'Autre Pied. A partnership between Aussie chef Shane Osborn and British front of house turned restaurateur David Moore, it was remodelled after a fire a couple of years ago. The long, narrow

"modern French cooking that makes the most of complicated combinations"

dining room is luxuriously cosy, the service seamless and the wine list made to match the ambitious menu. Osborn, follows in the footsteps of chefs Tom Aikens (see page 147) and Richard Neat, and has lasted longer than both without the tantrums, and achieved as much with his gimmick-free modern French cooking that makes the most of complicated combinations such as roast suckling pig, crackling, baby beetroot, pickled girolles and apple cider sauce.

34 Charlotte Street, Bloomsbury, W1T 2NH
Tel: 020 7636 1178   www.pied-a-terre.co.uk   £81
Open: 12.15–2.30pm, 6.15–11pm Mon–Fri; 6.15–11pm Sat

The Pig's Ear

British

Pub grub

This feels completely out of place in Chelsea, where the boozers tend to be either unapologetically unreconstructed or piss-poor attempts at gastropubs. The Pig's Ear, formerly The Front Page, is a laid-back operation (at times too laid back when it comes to the service) with a good line in gutsy pub grub. The spacious ground floor bar is all red Formica-topped tables, green vinyl upholstery, rock 'n' roll knick knacks on the walls and eponymous ale on draught. Lunchtimes are filled with laptop types making use of the free WiFi over a pint. The up-

stairs restaurant is a slightly more formal tableclothed affair set

"naturally big on bits of pig and other meaty treats, such as roast bone marrow"

in a cosy wooden-floored dining room. Both share the guts of a menu (there are a few more options upstairs) that's naturally big on bits of pig and other meaty treats, such as roast bone marrow.

35 Old Church Street, Chelsea, SW3 5BS
Tel: 020 7352 2908 www.thepigsear.co.uk   £37
Open: daily, noon–11pm (10.30pm Sun)

El Pirata

Frugal feasting

Tapas bars are fashionable again thanks in part to the
success of recent arrivals such as Barrafina (see page
26) and Dehesa (see page 59). All of which much have
raised a wry smiles from those behind the unpretentious
El Pirata, who have been serving up quality tapas and
warm Spanish hospitality over in Mayfair since 1994.
There's nothing trendy about the cooking here but
everything from the *croquetas* to the *crema catalana* is
well made and served with a smile. More substantial
main courses, such as generous helpings of suckling pig,

"there's nothing trendy about the cooking here"

are also available.
In an area not
renowned for af-
fordable options it's incredibly good value, in particular
their set lunch menu at £9.95 for two courses with a
glass of wine or beer. They've recently opened a new
hipper looking outlet over in W2 called El Pirata Deta-
pas.

5–6 Down Street, Mayfair, W1J 7AQ
Tel: 020 7491 3810 www.elpirata.co.uk   £35
Open: noon–11.30pm Mon–Fri; 6–11.30pm Sat

Map
C

Pizza Maletti

Italian

On-the-hoof/Frugal feasting

Take-away-only Soho pizza joint that offers possibly the best slice of pizza in London. Tremendously popular, Soho's film and TV runners and other assorted media types wait in the queue outside, that also contains the occasional furtive Soho shopper and the odd sussed off-the-beaten-track tourist. The on-the-hoof choice of Franceso Mazzei, chef proprietor of L'Anima (see page 18), who like everyone else comes for the fresh slices of traditionally topped thin crust pizza, cut into huge squares, and sold out by 3pm everyday. The salads, pasta dishes and

"possibly the best slice of pizza in London"

risottos are none too shabby either. Wash it down with a bitter orange S. Pellegrino and don't let it sit too long inside the paper bag before you take a bite or the topping will end up stuck to the inside. You really don't want that to happen with pizza this good.

26 Noel Street, Soho, W1F 8GY
Tel: 020 7439 4096 £5
Open: 10.30am–4.30pm. Closed Saturdays and Sundays.

Pomegranates

Clandestine rendezvous

Louche old Pimlico charmer that somehow seems preserved in time despite regulars, once 70s swingers, now moving towards death and incontinence, and a globetrotting menu that's as dated as the untouched, circa

"if these walls could talk, they'd probably have brought down a government or two"

1974 interior. An establishment where they still levy a cover charge and the dishes typically veer from old school French (crab *bisque* with oysters and Cognac) to Scandinavia (*gravadlax* with dill and mustard sauce) and even makes it over to Turkey via northeast Africa (*bureks* with Sudanese pepper sauce) and Jamaica (curried goat) before ending up back in Britain for a helping of treacle tart. Run by the evergreen proprietor Patrick Gwynn-Jones, a restaurateur who's given Westminster's finest (and a few of its worst) somewhere they still feel at home more than 30 years later. If these walls could talk, they'd probably have brought down a government or two.

94 Grosvenor Road, Pimlico SW1V 3LF
Tel: 020 7828 6565   £44
Open: 12.30–2.15pm, 7–11.15pm. Closed Sat lunch and Sun.

Map
C

Quo Vadis

British

Be pampered/Make an impression

The latest incarnation of Quo Vadis, a London Soho institution since 1926, is the work of the Hart Brothers, the Anglo-Iberian siblings behind the Spanish restaurants, Fino and Barrafina (see page 26). Previously Italian, the new Quo Vadis menu keeps things more British meets European with a mixture of quality meat (veal cutlet, various cuts of 28-day Hereford beef), pasta, roasted poultry such as squab and simply prepared

seafood. Upstairs, in the building where Marx (Karl not Groucho that is) once lived, the clubbable

"British meets European with a mixture of quality meat, pasta, roasted poultry and simply prepared fish"

Harts have opened a new members' club, where they'll probably let you go drinking until the small hours if you ask nicely. Back in the restaurant the increasingly dapper Eddie Hart is a consummately polite front-of-house type who, backed up by a keen young team, knows how to make his guests feel special.

26–29 Dean Street, Soho, W1D 3LL
Tel: 020 7437 9585 www.quovadissoho.co.uk   £51
Open: noon–2.45pm, 5.30–10.45pm. Closed Sundays.

Racine

French

Map
E

Clandestine rendezvous/Dine solo

Having returned from his time as a consultant with the Soho House group (see Café Boheme page 41) chef Henry Harris has recently re-taken possession of this classy Knightsbridge operation, first opened in 2002 in partnership with restaurant manager Eric Garnier. With its Parisian inspired interior and menu, it kick-started a trend for a return to the French bourgeois style (see page 69, Galvin Bistrot de Luxe) that everyone loved be-

"it kick-started a trend for the French bourgeois style that everyone loved"

fore it became de-valued by overex-tended and fake French brands such as Chez Gerard and Café Rouge. Harris is back in the kitchen doing what he does best with French classics from *tête de veau* (calf's head) to *petit pot au chocolat* and according to Michael Caine the best *steak au poivre* in London. What was some of the best service in London will recover after the departure of many of the front of house team, in the aftermath of a court case between Harris and Garnier.

239 Brompton Road, Knightsbridge, SW3 2EP
Tel: 020 7584 4477   £42
Open: noon–3pm (3.30pm Sat/Sun), 6–10.30pm (10pm Sun).

Ranoush Juice   Lebanese

Late night/On-the-hoof

Everyone bar vegetarians and meat-loving masochists comes here for the shawarma. The Middle Eastern answer to the döner kebab, the shawarma served at this outlet of the multi-faceted Maroush (see page 94) are arguably the best in London. Available in lamb, chicken or – if you don't have food combining issues – mixed. They come tidily wrapped in fat, fresh pita packed with juicy, fragrant flesh, salad and – unless you decline, which would be a mistake – a generous slavering of garlic yoghurt, with the emphasis on the garlic. Wash it down with a fresh melon juice or lemonade and don't dwell on the occasionally surly but always efficient service. Although there are a select number of shiny metal seats available, most stumble out, *shawarma* in hand, to drip garlic sauce down their front as they take in the wonders of Edgware Road at night.

"fat, fresh pita packed with juicy, fragrant flesh, salad and a generous slavering of garlic yoghurt"

43 Edgware Road, London, W2 2JR
Tel: 020 7723 5929 www.maroush.com   £35
Open: daily, 9am–3am

Rasa

Frugal feasting/On-the-hoof/Worth the schlep

The original and best branch of what's now a wide-spread group of London restaurants, this small hot-pink-painted, incense burning, Stoke Newington South Indian has, unlike some of the other Rasas (including the excellent Rasa Travancore opposite), that have branched out into meat and seafood, stuck to its authentic, all-vegetarian Kerala-Hindu-inspired menu. Owner Das Sreedharan, who grew up in Cochin and moved to London to study accountancy, only to open this, his first restaurant, in 1994, has dedicated a cookbook to his loyal Stokey locals. One of

"authentic, all-vegetarian Kerala-Hindu-inspired menu"

whom is Morgan Meunier, chef proprietor of Morgan M in Islington, who likes to take his family there for an affordable meal that can start with *masala vadai* (deep-fried lentil patties) and move on to *nair dosas* (pancakes filled with potatoes, beetroot and carrots) and *cheera* curry before finishing with *pal payasam* – rice pudding with cashews and raisins.

55 Stoke Newington Church Street, Dalston, N16 0AR
Tel: 020 7249 0344 www.rasarestaurants.com   £26
Open: noon–3pm (Sat/Sun only), 6–10.45pm (11.30pm Fri/Sat)

Restaurant Gordon Ramsay

Modern french

Be pampered/When someone else pays

They've given up pretending that Ramsay himself spends much time in the kitchen here anymore. Nowadays he's everywhere – mostly getting his highlights done down at the salon or swearing on television. But whether he's there or not, Ramsay's Chelsea flagship looks like it's in safe hands after the recent appointment of no-nonsense Northern Irish head chef Clare Smyth. The cooking's about luxury ingredients and technical brilliance in dishes such as line-caught turbot fillet stud-

ded with Perigord truffle, *boulangère* potatoes, leek *ballotine* and civet

"the service, under Jean-Claude Breton, is undoubtedly some of the best in London"

sauce. The interior, redone a couple of years ago, is not exactly riveting, the wine list is suitably grand and the service, under Jean-Claude Breton, is undoubtedly some of the best in London. As you'd expect, tables are hard to come by at short notice unless you're in Ramsay's good books – and it's stonkingly expensive.

68 Royal Hospital Road, Chelsea, SW3 4HP
Tel: 020 7352 4441   www.gordonramsay.com   £102
Open: noon–2.30pm, 6.30–11pm Mon–Fri

The River Café

Modern Italian

**Be pampered/Lazy Sunday/Make an impression/People watch/Quintessential London/
/When someone else pays**

Celebrating your 20th year in business with a kitchen fire (rumour has it a chef got a bit cocky cooking a steak) that, combined with planned refurbishment work, closed you down for five months is a strange way to spend your birthday. But that's how it went down recently for Hammersmith's ever-popular River Café, opened in 1988, and now back up and running and looking as lovely as ever after a makeover. Imagine the best Italian produce mon-

"the best Italian produce money can buy"

ey can buy, a cost they unfortunately pass on to the customer, perfectly assembled, served in a modern glass fronted canteen, down where the old Thames does flow. Perfect setting, meets perfect produce, meets educated service and a wine list, aside from odd Champagne, that is all Italian with, assuming you stay away from the Super Tuscans, lots of bottles under £30.

Thames Wharf, Rainville Road. Hammersmith, W6

Tel: 020 7386 4200 www.rivercafe.co.uk   **£63**
Open: 12.30 (noon Sun)–2.15pm (2.30pm Sat, 3pm Sun), 7–11pm (11.20pm Fri/Sat). Closed Sun dinner.

Rochelle Canteen

British

Worth the schlep

A Monday to Friday lunchtime Shoreditch operation, housed in what were once bike sheds for a Victorian school, which now operates as studios for designers and artists. In addition to acting as the canteen for the near-by arty souls, it's also a destination for some because of the involvement of Margot Henderson, wife of Fergus Henderson of St John, (see page 133) who also runs a catering company with Melanie Arnold out of the aforementioned sheds. In the warmer months there are tables outside in what was the school's playground, as well as in the noisy kitchen-shed-cum-canteen. A bring your own booze affair, unless you fancy ginger beer, the short, daily-changing menu takes a similar nose-to-tail, seasonal British approach as St John but charges a lot less for dishes such as smoked mackerel, dandelion and horseradish salad or gooseberry fool.

"the short, daily-changing menu takes a similar nose-to-tail, seasonal British approach as St John"

School House, Arnold Circus, Shoreditch, E2 7ES
Tel: 020 7729 5677   www.arnoldandhenderson.com   £28
Open: noon–3pm Mon–Fri

Roka

Clandestine rendezvous/Dine solo/Wish they'd thought of it

The fact that it's well on its way to becoming a global brand, with branches in the US and the Far East, hasn't stopped this, German chef Reiner Becker's original *robata* grill joint, from jumping. Sister restaurant to upscale Knightsbridge sushi emporium Zuma (see page 163), it's built around a central dining counter, made out of a huge slab of handsomely gnarled wood, behind which various fish, meat and poultry are expertly cooked over an open flame. The rest of the menu is mostly made up

"fish, meat and poultry are expertly cooked over an open flame"

of sushi, in its various guises, and *sashimi*. The sake list is lengthy and the service is keen and helpful. The buzzing atmosphere means it's the perfect place to grab a seat at the sushi bar and dine alone, if you're lucky next to Trinity chef Adam Byatt doing the same. Beneath Roka sits the Shochu Lounge, a sexily lit basement bar and lounge with a cocktail list that calls heavily on the Japanese spirit, hidden nooks and crannies for canoodling aplenty and the full Roka menu available.

37 Charlotte Street, Bloomsbury, W1T 1RR
Tel: 020 7580 6464 www.rokarestaurant.com   £69
Open: noon (12.30pm Sat/Sun)–3.30pm, 5.30–11.30pm.
Closed Sunday dinner.

Royal China

Cantonese

Be pampered/Clandestine rendezvous/Frugal feasting/Lazy Sunday/On-the-hoof

There are arguments in favour of most members of the six-strong, Hong Kong-owned, Royal China group, but in terms of chefs, (Henry Harris, Heston Blumenthal, Ichiro Kubota) and critics, (Fay Maschler, Zoe Williams) affections it comes down to a toss up between the Royal China Club in Baker Street, and the original Royal China in Queensway. The Cantonese cooking at both is excellent, if conservative. While the former is more modern, less shiny and in some ways slicker, Royal China at the Hyde Park end of Queensway, the most lauded Chinese in Bayswater, wins out for the

"glitzy, 80s black and gold interior that feels like a Macau casino from an old Bond film"

sheer sheen of its cavernous, glitzy, 80s black and gold interior that feels like a Macau casino from an old Bond film circa Roger Moore. It's a room that somehow muffles the noise even when it's packed full of enthusiastic dim sum diners as it is most lunchtimes and especially on a Sunday.

13 Queensway, Bayswater, W2 4QJ
Tel: 020 7221 2435 www.rcguk.hk   £38
Open: noon (11am Sun)–11pm (11.30pm Fri/Sat, 10pm Sun)

RSJ

Abuse the wine list/Clandestine rendezvous

Long running discreet South Bank destination by way of
Waterloo, that opened in converted 19th-century stables
(named after the rolled steel joints used to hold up its
roof) back in 1980. The cooking is French on the whole,
but takes in Mediterranean influences and likes to make

use of name-
checked seasonal
British ingredients.
An approach seen
in dishes such as
Italian pale
aubergine, ricotta,
oregano, penne
pasta; roast Suf-
folk lamb, French
beans, baby fennel
and finger carrots;
and Lemon curd
tartlet with fresh
summer berries.
The wine list, a
favourite of Hes-
ton Blumenthal, is
a long love letter
to the Loire Valley,
with the 250 or so
different bins from
the region. "Being
shallow I like to

*"I like to try lots of different
wines in rapid succession. Their
entry level list of dozen wines
by the glass lets me do that"*
— Caroline Stacey

try lots of different wines in rapid succession," notes
food writer, Caroline Stacey, "Their entry level list of
dozen wines by the glass lets me do that."

33 Coin Street, Waterloo, SE1 9NR
Tel: 020 7928 4554 www.rsj.uk.com   £41
Open: noon–2.30pm, 5.30–11pm. Closed Sat lunch and
Sunday.

Sagar

Indian vegetarian

Frugal feasting/On-the-hoof

This Hammersmith vegetarian specialises in South Indian home-style dishes. Housed in a smart, modern-looking dining room fronted with huge glass panes, it's a friendly place and popular with everyone from Indian families, to students and sorts who look like refuges from the River Café (see page 119). The service tends to lose the plot when it gets a bit too busy, making it an ideal weekday lunch venue. It's very reasonably priced, so much so that it's the frugal feasting choice of Charles Campion, editor of the *London Restaurant Guide*, who declares it a purveyor of "satisfying South Indian vegetarian cooking". Everything – from

"Satisfying South Indian cooking"
– Charles Campion

the opening offers of *dosas*, *samosas* and *vadas* (lentil doughnuts) to main courses of *kootus* made with fresh coconut and yoghurt, and chickpea curry to sides of rice cakes – is produced to a standard that belies the low cost.

157 King Street, Hammersmith, W6 9JT
Tel: 020 8741 8563
£24
Open: noon–2.45pm, 5.30–10.45pm (Fri 11.30pm) Mon–Fri; noon–10.45pm Sat/Sun

Sake No Hana

Make an impression/When someone else pays

Alan Yau, of Hakkasan (see page 75) and Yauatcha (see page 162) fame, recently transformed this tricky Modernist 1960s St James' office building into a luxurious Japanese restaurant. The ground floor sushi bar is understated, not so the first floor restaurant, which you ascend to, via a tunnel of listed escalator encased in a series of shiny black panels. Suspended from the ceiling hang giant Jenga-like formations of wooden blocks, while the recessed traditional-style seating (there are some tables also) with *tatami* mats is not designed for

showing off killer heels. The menu is a complicated arrangement of small appetisers,

"recessed traditional-style seating with tatami mats is not designed for showing off killer heels"

sushi, *sashimi*, *tempura* and larger braised dishes, and, unless you're very well up on your Japanese food, you'll need help ordering from the waiting staff. There's a seriously extensive sake list but an accomplished sake sommelier always on hand to guide you.

23 St James's Street, Mayfair, SW1A 1HA
Tel: 020 7925 8988   £84
Open: daily, noon–3pm, 6pm–midnight (11pm Sun)

Scott's

Seafood

Dine solo/Make an impression/People watch

Say what you will about Richard Caring, rag-trade millionaire turned aggressively acquisitive restaurateur, but few would have had the readies to restore this classic Mount Street oyster bar and fish restaurant. Its relaunch in December 2006 cost an estimated £5 million, with £1 million spent on a new air conditioning system that was a feat of modern engineering, with two 150 metre bore holes drilled down to London's water table. The menu's

a lot simpler, working its way through every sort of shellfish you can imagine be-

"cadge a seat at the green onyx topped oyster bar, guzzle some oysters and champagne, and view all the goings-on"

fore moving on to main courses such as grilled Dover sole and lobster thermidor. Once past Sean McDermott, London's greatest doorman, see if you can cadge a seat at the green onyx topped oyster bar, guzzle some oysters and champagne, and view all the goings-on in the bustling, increasingly star-studded, oak-panelled dining room.

20 Mount Street, Mayfair, W1K 2HE
Tel: 020 7495 7309 www.scotts-restaurant.com
£59
Open: daily, noon–10.30pm (10pm Sun)

Shampers

Time warp wine bar

Map C

Abuse the wine list/Dine solo

This 80s throwback (it actually opened in 1977) is the sort of wine bar that used to be a ubiquitous feature of London life. That it's survived where many others have sunk without trace in a sea of mediocre Beaujolais Nouveau is a testament to Shampers staying power. A good location has helped, as has an unpretentious well-priced menu that does comfort via a mix of duck confit, steak sandwiches and steak and kidney pie. Naturally the well-priced wine list that tours the world but spends the most

time in France, much like the menu, has played its part. As the

"it's survived where many others have sunk without trace in a sea of mediocre Beaujolais Nouveau"

name would suggest, there's a particularly good selection of champagne, and pudding wines and ports. Run by the same proprietor since the mid 80s, it's popular with aging Soho advertising types and bufferish bores – but don't let that put you off.

4 Kingly Street, Soho, W1R 5LF
Tel: 020 7437 1692 www.shampers.net

£41

Open: 11am–11pm. Closed Sundays.

Sketch

Modern French

Be pampered/Make an impression/When someone else pays

The jaw-dropping effect that Sketch has on first-timers has not diminished since it opened in 2002. The brainchild of Mourad 'Momo' Mazouz, who signed up French superstar chef Pierre Gagnaire, Sketch immediately got a reputation for being expensive, both for the £12m it cost to renovate its Grade II listed building and for the cost of a meal in its upstairs Lecture Room restaurant. So much so that open-topped tour buses now stop outside to tell tourists about 'London's most expensive restaurant'. All of which is a little unfair, especially since Sketch is so much more than a restaurant, consisting of, as it does, two restau-

"Sketch is so much more than a restaurant"

rants, two bars, an art gallery and a patisserie, and if you eat at night downstairs in the Gallery surrounded by video art, or in the daytime in the patisserie, it's really not that pricey.

9 Conduit Street, Mayfair, W1S 2XG
Tel: 020 7659 4500   £58
Open: 8am (10am Sat)–2am. Closed Sundays.

Snazz Sichuan

Dine solo

There are two ways to approach the latest Sichuan specialist to arrive in London following the opening of Bar Shu (see page 25). First, fly solo, feel your way around the unfamiliar fiery Sichuanese menu. That done, return with your most forward thinking food-loving friends and

"predictably high on chilli and numbing sichuan pepper, ... not afraid of unusually textured bits of offal"

give them an edited tour of a collection of dishes, predictably high on chilli and numbing Sichuan pepper, that's not afraid of unusually textured bits of offal. Part of the New China Club, which, set over two floors near Euston also comprises a teahouse and an art gallery, the fun, gaudily decorated dining room aims to promote Sichuanese culture. Cold dishes include ox tripe, pig's ear and 'strange-flavour' rabbit. Moving on there's 'fish-fragrant' pork slivers, 'fire-exploded' kidney flowers, 'special cooked pig blood casserole' and 'fragrant-and-spicy' duck tongues, to name but a few of the challenges the menu presents.

37 Charlton Street, Euston, NW1 1JD
Tel: 020 7388 0808 www.newchinaclub.co.uk   £38
Open: daily, noon–11.30pm

Sông Quê   Vietnamese

Frugal feasting

In the heart of the Little Vietnam that this stretch of
Hackney's Kingsland Road represents, Sông Quê has a
vast menu – one that hides in bits and pieces of heavily
sauced Cantonese dishes among Vietnamese *pho*, noodle and rice assemblies and authentically light and fragrant seafood and meat dishes. The service is hit and
miss at times, as is the cooking, but it's stupidly cheap,
the *pho*, for example, easily a meal in itself. They come

with bowls of
raw bean shoots
and basil leaves,
that you add as

*"Eat till you bust and the waiters
are laughing at you for about £20
a head" – Marina O'Loughlin*

required, to bulk up your basic broth of rice noodles, co-
riander and onion, plus whatever protein you've
plumped for in the one of 20-odd varieties on offer. As
Marina O'Loughlin, restaurant critic of *Metro*, puts it,
"Eat till you bust and the waiters are laughing at you for
about £20 a head."

134 Kingsland Road, Hackney, E2 8DY
Tel: 020 7613 3222   £22
Open: noon–3pm, 5.30–11pm Mon–Sat; noon–11pm Sun

The Square

Modern French

Abuse the wine list/Be pampered/Make an impression/When someone else pays/Wish they'd thought of it

There was a time when they called him Nigel 'The Square' Platts-Martin but the truth is the restaurateur behind this haute Mayfair operation – and La Trompette (see page 151) and Chez Bruce (see page 48) – knows The Square is really about his partnership with chef Phillip Howard. They've just celebrated a decade in Bruton Street, having originally opened in King Street St James' back in 1991. Howard's cooking, which keeps things modern French, is some of London's finest in dishes such as the shared whole roast

"less of a list, more of a beautifully chosen War and Peace of wine" – Tom Parker Bowles

monkfish tail with girolles, herb macaroni and garlic. Shame a lot of it's wasted feeding the suits on expenses. As for the celebrated wine list, food writer Tom Parker Bowles declares it "less of a list and more of a beautifully chosen War and Peace of wine."

6–10 Bruton Street, Mayfair, W1J 6PU

Tel: 020 7495 7100   www.squarerestaurant.org   £82
Open: noon–2.30pm, 6.30–10pm (10.30pm Sat, 9.30pm Sun). Closed Sat/Sun lunch.

Map
C

St Alban
Mediterranean

Abuse the wine list/Make an impression/ People watch

The seasoned restaurateur team of Chris Corbin and Jeremy King tried to do something completely different following the success of the nearby Wolseley (see page 159). They embraced the modern for the first time in a space with a low-slung ceiling and the sort of curves that make it look like the vision of what an airport lounge should be, lifted straight from the pages of *Wallpaper**. Launched by chef Francesco Mazzei before he left to open L'Anima (see page 18), the upscale menu cruises around the Mediterranean. The wine list accordingly takes in bottles from around France, Spain, Italy and Portugal. Food writer Caroline Stacey has the people-watching

"clock everyone from WAG wannabes in backless dresses to Harold Pinter and Antonia Fraser" – Caroline Stacey

opportunities as ripe, thanks to the "low banquettes that offer an uninterrupted outlook" and reckons you can "clock everyone from WAG wannabes in backless dresses to Harold Pinter and Antonia Fraser".

Rex House, 4–12 Regent Street, Piccadilly, SW1Y 4PE
Tel: 020 7499 8558   www.stalban.net   £46
Open: daily, noon–3.30pm, 5.30pm–midnight (11pm Sun)

St John

Dine solo/Make an impression/Quintessential London

Recently freshly whitewashed, don't expect any other great changes at Trevor Gulliver and chef Fergus Henderson's seminal St John, opened back in 1994 and named after the Clerkenwell street it stands on. The influence of this famed 'nose-to-tail' modern British eating emporium, opened in an old smokehouse in the shadow of Smithfield meat market, can be felt in restaurants

"famed nose-to-tail modern British eating emporium"

such as Hereford Road (see page 76), Market (see page 93), the Anchor & Hope (see page 14) and Rochelle Canteen (see page 120). Tersely written, the strictly seasonal, twice-daily changing menu typically takes in such things as langoustines with mayonnaise, chitterlings and strawberry Eton mess. The service comes from a knowledgeable young team, while proprietor Trevor Gulliver is fond of his French wine, something reflected on his list, with nowhere but France getting a look-in and the own-label house red, white and champagne.

26 St John Street, Clerkenwell, EC1M 4AY
Tel: 020 7251 0848   www.stjohnrestaurant.com   £44
Open: noon–3pm, 6–11pm Mon–Fri; 6–11pm Sat

St John Bread & Wine British

Breakfast

Offshoot of St John (see page 133) opened in 2003 over by Spitalfields Market, built around a bakery and a wine shop, with a staggered menu that runs all day from breakfast to dinner, reflecting the British seasonal St John approach but more tailored to tapas-style sharing. A typical day might start with an Old Spot bacon sandwich, have an elevenses of some seed cake and a glass of Madeira — my dear, pop in at lunch for some smoked

"A typical day might start with an Old Spot bacon sandwich"

sprats and horse-radish, followed by duck and lentils. Finish the day with a dinner of pigeon and hispi, with Eccles cake & Lancashire cheese for afters. The all-white interior has an open kitchen and bakery at the back and chairs that tend to numb the bum. The wine list, as at St John, is one for the Francophiles.

94–96 Commercial Street, Shoreditch, E1 6LZ
Tel: 020 7251 0848   www.stjohnbreadandwine.com   £30
Open: daily, 9am (10am Sat/Sun)–11pm (10.30pm Sun)

St John's

Mediterranean

Lazy Sunday/Pub grub/Worth the schlep

Not to be confused with St John (see page 133) this old Archway boozer, in a perennially up and coming neighbourhood, was once the centre of the Irish community. It's a beautiful looking pub with a bronzed ceiling, chandeliers, plush banquettes and lots of portraits on the leafy-green walls. There's still Guinness behind the bar, as well a decent choice of ale, bitter and wheat beer. The small kitchen, at the back of the pleasingly old

"everbody raves incessantly about the pavlova"

school dining room, keeps it seasonal while veering between Mediterranean-tinged dishes, such as octopus and chickpea stew, and the infinitely more British, and reminiscent of the other St John (that you're not supposed to be confusing it with), ox tongue with pickled walnuts and cauliflower. Desserts are particularly comforting British-inspired efforts such as greengage ripple ice cream with biscuits and everybody raves incessantly about their pavlova.

91 Junction Road, Archway, N19 5QU
Tel: 020 7272 1587   £27
Open: daily, noon–11pm

St Pancras Champagne Bar

Bar

Clandestine rendezvous/Quintessential London

Don't believe the hype, the rebuilt St Pancras is not New York's Grand Central Station. But, aside from being able to catch a train that will take you to Paris in just over 2 hours, the one thing that St Pancras can boast about is this champagne bar. Run by Searcy it seats 110 along the Eurostar platform in a series of leather-upholstered banquettes, with art deco styled lamps and built-in heaters, to take the chill off when it's cold. There are 70 different champagnes on offer, starting at £42 and rising to £940 for a magnum of Louis Roederer Cristal. The menu sells simple luxury to go with the champagne, from

"The menu sells simple luxury to go with the champagne"

smoked salmon and scrambled eggs for breakfast, to caviar for elevenses and beyond. According to chef Richard Corrigan, this is his go-to for a clandestine 'Brief Encounter' rendezvous.

St Pancras International Station, St Pancras, NW1
Tel: 020 7843 4250   www.stpancras.com/drink   £44
Open: daily, 8am–11pm

Sushi Hiro

Clandestine rendezvous/On-the-hoof/Worth the schlep

It's no insult to the good people of Ealing that this low-key but exceptional sushi bar seems a bit out of place in an arse end West London suburb – no offence. But then again as the so-called 'Queen of suburbs' has in its midst a sizeable Japanese community, it makes sense they should have some-where worthy of their national cuisine to eat in – and takeaway from – nearby. The service is a bit chaotic but there's nothing wrong with the superb sushi, according to its fan club that includes Heston Blumenthal of The Fat Duck, Henry Harris of Racine (see page 115) and restaurateur Oliver Peyton, who all believe the trip out to this neck of the

"its fan club that includes Heston Blumenthal, Henry Harris and Oliver Peyton"

woods is well worth the effort. The affordable menu of sushi and *sashimi* ticks all the boxes, while you have to tick lots of boxes too – with a pencil on the paper menu slip you're given on a small clipboard.

1 Station Parade, Uxbridge Road, Ealing, W5 3LD
Tel: 020 8896 3175   £35
Open: 11am–1.30pm, 4.30–9pm. Closed Mondays.

Sushi Say

Japanese

On-the-hoof/Worth the schlep

On a par with similar suburban hero, Sushi-Hiro (see
page 137), Willesden's Sushi Say is an excellent Japanese in an unexpected location. Family run by a seasoned
husband and wife team, he makes much of the sushi,
she busies herself in the dining room, it's a typically
compact little number – 10 seats around the sushi bar
and another 20 in the restaurant. There's every sushi option, from *nigiri* to all the usual shapes and sizes of roll,
generously done, with no skimping on the high quality
fish when it comes to the *sashimi*. The menu of specials,
such as *kabocha no netsuke* – mirin and sake stewed
pumpkin, rotates regularly with the seasons. Of particu-

lar interest to fans
and follower's of
sake is the pres-

*"enjoy sake as a half-frozen
slush-puppy"*

ence of Akita Onigoroshi, a gimmicky, but deliciously re-
freshing way to enjoy sake as a half-frozen slush-puppy.

33b Walm Lane, Willesden, NW2 5SH
Tel: 020 8459 7512   £35
Open: noon–2pm, 6.30–10pm Tues–Fri; 1–3pm, 6–10.30pm
Sat; 1–3pm, 6–9.30pm Sun

Sweetings

Quintessential London

Old school city fish restaurant that's been operating on the same site since 1889, which safely qualifies it for being described as both an institution and a bastion of tradition. Sweetings only opens for lunch from Monday to Friday, always has done. A singularly spartan space, save for its mosaic-tiled floor, it fills up quickly when the doors open at 11.30am. The City gents that go there regularly, do so to perch uncomfortably on stools at its counters and order from the all-seafood menu that usually includes oysters, potted shrimps, smoked eel whitebait, herring roe, smoked haddock, fish pie and skate. The wine list is brutally short and French, while other alcoholic options include Guinness and bitter served in pewter tankards. Puddings are nostalgic and British, with crumble and spotted dick always making an appearance.

"both an institution and a bastion of tradition"

39 Queen Victoria Street, City, EC4N 4SA
Tel: 020 7248 3062   £39
Open: 11.30am–3pm. Closed Saturdays and Sundays.

Tamarind

Indian

Be pampered/Make an impression

This Mayfair basement has been leading the way for haute Indian in London since 1995. Atul Kochhar, its award-winning opening head chef for six years until 2001, went on to open Benares (see page 29). But Alfred Prasad has since stepped into his shoes and made his own name with a menu that focuses on the tandoor oven and traditional Moghul dishes. Tamarind's success is built on the accomplished cooking in dishes such as succulent *lasooni pasliyan* (grilled lamb cutlets seasoned with garlic, chilli, lime and cumin and topped with

aubergine) and a melting *seekh kabab* (skewers of

"Tamarind's success is built on the accomplished cooking"

spiced ground lamb). Seasonal lunch menus offer a way in for those on a budget otherwise it's expensive. But for the price you also get some of the best service in London, always friendly and efficient, under the watchful eye of the ever-suave Rajesh Suri.

20 Queen Street, Mayfair, W1J 5PR
Tel: 020 7629 3561 www.tamarindrestaurant.com   £43
Open: noon–2.45pm, 6 (6.30pm Sun)–11.15pm (10.30pm Sun). Closed Saturday lunch.

Taro

Frugal feasting/On-the-hoof

Mr Taro, it's his face on the sign outside, knows that the secret to making money feeding people in Soho is in quick, affordable meals with a fast turnaround in clean, simple surroundings. It's a formula that's worked so well

for Taro that they've recently opened a second Soho branch of this, their no-nonsense, cheap and cheery, Japanese proposition on Old Compton Street. It's laid out like a simple café, the seats a little cramped, the leg room not quite there at the sushi bar. The service is swift and friendly, the sushi so-so. The one-bowl meals like the *ramen* and *teriyaki* are a better bet, both in terms of

"quick, affordable meals with a fast turnaround in clean, simple surroundings"

quality and value. Not a place to linger perhaps – staff will expect you to be done and dusted well within an hour – but an excellent Soho stop-off nonetheless.

61 Brewer Street, Soho, W1F 9UW
Tel: 020 7794 0190 £24
Open: noon–2.30pm, 6–11pm

Tayyabs

Indian

Frugal feasting/Quintessential London

There's only one curry house in the East End where they queue around the block for a table – New Tayyab in Whitechapel. Opened back in 1974 by Mohammad Tayyab, the decades saw it expand from a café and move into the former corner pub site that it now occupies. The simple menu of excellent Punjabi dry-meat curries, buttery breads and some exemplary tandoor dishes in chicken and mutton *tikka*, *seekh* and *shami* kebabs and deep-marinated lamb chops is all priced so cheaply, says, Jay Rayner, the *Observer*'s restaurant critic, "that they practically pay you to take the food away". While Charles Campion

"they practically pay you to take the food away" – Jay Rayner

also gives it the nod, for being a multi-cultural London experience like no other, "What could be better than a Pakistani grill house?" he asks. Unlicensed, it's a BYO deal, which keeps the cost down even more.

83–89 Fieldgate Street, Whitechapel, E1 1JU
Tel: 020 7247 6400 www.tayyabs.co.uk   £18
Open: daily, noon–midnight

The Terrace

Breakfast/Clandestine rendezvous

Concealed within London's oldest square, leafy Lincoln's Inn Fields near Holborn, this restaurant run by chef Patrick William, that's only open for breakfast and lunch, Monday to Friday, is an unexpected treat. Williams has trained and cooked alongside some of the best, including Marco Pierre White, and combines his classic French training with a little of his Caribbean roots. He'll start your day with a 'Caribbean Big Breakfast' if you

"combines his classic French training with a little of his Caribbean roots"

ask him – the usual fry-up components with the addition of sweet potato and fried plantain. Then at lunch, assuming you've worked that off, he'll do you jerk chicken and *pancetta* Caesar salad, followed by *panacotta* with deep fried banana. They have an outside terrace for dining on come the sunshine, while the rest of the year you sit inside a pleasant wood-framed glass-sided structure. The perfect secluded setting for an off-the-beaten-track lunch.

Lincoln's Inn Fields, Holborn, WC2A 3LJ
Tel: 020 7430 1234 www.theterrace.info   £31
Open: 8am–9pm Mon–Fri

Theo Randall Italian

When someone else pays

The man who did most of the cooking at the River Café (see page 119) for years has now got his name on the door of this dining room at Park Lane's Intercontinental. The room is a bit of an unlovable mutt – expensively decked-out but still somehow soulless. Not so Randall's cooking, which has enough soul to fill the room by focusing on the finest seasonal ingredients prepared the Italian way, simply dressed and perfectly cooked. The service, unlike the site, doesn't let the side down and, although picked by the evergreen, bearded restaurant consultant Roy Ackerman, as where to go when

"finest seasonal ingredients prepared the Italian way, simply dressed and perfectly cooked"

someone else is footing the bill, it's considerably cheaper than the River Café. All of it gives you more firepower for the well-chosen wine list. Now, if only they could do something with that room, Randall's cooking deserves it.

InterContinental London, 1 Hamilton Place, Park Lane, W1J 7QY
Tel: 020 7318 8747 www.theorandall.com £55
Open: noon–3pm, 6–11pm Mon–Fri; 6–11pm Sat

Tokyo Diner

Late night

Quirky little Japanese joint on the edge of Chinatown, that's been going since 1992. You enter through a sliding door, the ground floor dining room a series of spartan benches and tables. Although they serve *maki* and *nigiri*

"you will not find any kind of tuna listed, a stance taken in response to concerns about overfishing and sustainability"

sushi, unusually for a Japanese restaurant, you will not find any kind of tuna listed, a stance taken in response to concerns about over-fishing and sustainability. The main focus of the menu is simple cooked dishes such as *katsu don*, breaded pork over rice, and o*yako don*, 'parent and child' – a mixture of chicken, soft-cooked egg and spring onion. There are also noodle dishes such as curry *udon* and *bento* boxes of chicken or salmon *teriyaki*. On the way out you're confronted with another Tokyo Diner quirk, they don't accept tips be-cause – as they explain – in Japan it's not the custom.

2 Newport Place, Leicester Square, WC2H 7JP
Tel: 020 7287 8777 www.tokyodiner.com   £23
Open: daily, noon–midnight

Tom Aikens

Modern French

Be pampered/Make an impression

Tom Aikens' takeover of this corner of Chelsea began here in 2003, with the opening of this his eponymous flagship. These days he's got the casual Tom's Kitchen just around the corner and the recently opened posh-chippie Tom's Place, across the way. But it's his signature restaurant that is still his true love. Open only Monday to Friday, it's a polished haute experience in an elegant modern dining room, the service seamless, and a special mention going to Gearoid Devaney, one of the most affably knowledge-able sommeliers in London. Then there's the cook-ing, which, as Aikens has started to relax and enjoy his success, seems less intense, less showy and more enjoyable for all

"a polished haute experience in an elegant modern dining room"

concerned. Respected by fellow chefs, Aikens is some-where chef Jason Atherton routinely takes friends to make an impression on them. It's predictably expensive, but the set lunch at £29 for three courses won't break the bank – just don't let that sommelier charm you.

43 Elystan Street, Chelsea, SW3 3NT
Tel: 020 7584 2003   www.tomaikens.co.uk   £68
Open: noon–2.30pm, 6.45–10.30pm. Closed Sat and Sun.

Tom Ilic

Modern European

Frugal feasting/Worth the schlep

A new Battersea home for talented Serbian chef Tom Ilic, who was last seen in the kitchen at Addendum, a
rather flash hotel restaurant, near Tower Bridge. But he
seems much more at home here on the Queenstown
Road, where he can concentrate on his cooking. He likes
cooking meat in particular and seems to have a thing
about pigs, there's a little piggy sticking its head out of
the 'O' in his name on his restaurant's logo. Then there
was the recent dish on the menu that featured not a trio
of pork but pork prepared five-ways. So not a chef to

take your favourite
vegetarian aunt to –
but one that's well

*"not a chef to take your
favourite vegetarian aunt to"*

worth the journey to Battersea, particularly as he's offering a two-course lunch, with cooking of a standard that
should be somewhere much grander, but thankfully isn't,
for £12.50.

123 Queenstown Rd, Battersea, SW8 3RH

Tel: 020 7622 0555 www.tomilic.com   £35
Open: noon–2.30pm Weds–Fri, noon–3.30pm Sun;
6–10.30pm Tues–Sat.

Tom's Deli

Delicatessen

Breakfast/Dine solo

A Westbourne Grove stalwart, Tom's Deli does exactly what it says on the awning. First and foremost a deli, Tom's is devoted to sourcing and sells all sorts of expensive goodies: charcuterie, cheeses, olives, biscuits, cakes and overpriced soft drinks. Part of Tom Conran's mini-Empire that includes the nearby Cow (see page 56), Crazy Homies (see page 57) and Lucky 7 (see page 90), it's the small, friendly café at the back that's the real

draw. In among the pricey boutiques of – save for the Post Office – the over-gentri-

"always packed with off-duty Notting Hillbillies, fumbling with their phones and gossiping over a long, late breakfast

fied Westbourne Grove, it's always packed with off-duty Notting Hillbillies, fumbling with their phones and gossiping over a long, late breakfast. It can be a pain trying to get a table and the service is sometimes as flaky as a butter croissant but Continental, British or American, all the breakfast options are here.

226 Westbourne Grove, Notting Hill, W11 2RH
Tel: 020 7221 8818   www.tomsdelilondon.co.uk   £23
Open: daily, 8am (9am Sun)–5.30pm (6.30pm Sat/Sun)

Trader Vic's  60s Polynesian kitsch

Clandestine rendezvous

Plying its trade in the bowels of Park Lane Hilton since 1963, the tiki-themed Trader Vic's is in part the inspiration behind Mahiki, the camp Mayfair cocktail bar that briefly found fame as a hangout for young Royals. But Trader Vic's is much more entertaining. It's staffed by waitresses who are pure gone-to-seed glamour in cling-fit Polynesian gowns and bartenders in Hawaiian shirts who look like reluctant extras from a *Lost* episode or *Magnum PI* as they scowl to a piped Polynesian soundtrack. Forget the vaguely aloha-themed food unless you want something to soak up cocktails served in ceramic coconuts, barrels, bowls and the like. Which – after a couple of Samoan

"pure gone-to-seed glamour in Polynesian cling-fit gowns"

Fog Cutters – you will. Fay Maschler, restaurant critic, *The Evening Standard*, has it down as perfect for a clandestine rendezvous and asks, "Did anyone know it was still trading?"

The London Hilton, 22 Park Lane, Mayfair, W1Y 1BE
Tel: 020 7221 8818 www.tradervicslondon.com £54
Open: noon–5pm, 6pm–12.30am Mon–Fri; 6pm–12.30am Sat

Trinity Modern European

Worth the schlep

Adam Byatt returned to south London and Clapham in 2006 to open Trinity not far from where he'd opened his first restaurant, Thyme. A triumphant homecoming, after a difficult time in the West End, Trinity is the sort of accomplished, well-priced local restaurant everyone wishes they had on their doorstep. The dining room, decked out in chocolate and cream, is handsome, the service sweet and the wine list well pitched. Byatt meanwhile has stepped back from the small plate shtick he practised back in Thyme, although he still does a tasting menu, and these days instead does much of

"the sort of accomplished, well-priced local restaurant everyone wishes they had on their doorstep"

his cooking within a traditionally structured à la carte, be it complex combinations such as roast rump and sweetbreads of rose veal with grain mustard *choucroute*, runner beans and truffled cauliflower cheese; or twisted classics in fig tarte tatin with mascarpone sorbet.

4 The Polygon, Clapham, SW4 0JG
Tel: 020 7622 1199   www.trinityrestaurant.co.uk £43
Open: 12.30–2.30pm (3pm Sun), 6.30–10.30pm. Closed Monday lunch.

La Trompette

Abuse the wine list/Be pampered/Worth the schlep

With a head chef in James Bennington who cut his kitchen teeth with Bruce Poole at Chez Bruce (see page 48), which along with The Square (see page 131) is also owned by restaurateur Nigel Platts-Martin, this is very

much a polished modern French affair. The restrained dining room, all neutral tones, is filled with Chiswick's most affluent and the likes of Tom Pemberton who venture this far West for the critically praised cooking in dishes such as suckling pig ravioli and roast sea bass with olive oil mash. It's served by a front of house team with silky smooth skills

"topped off with a wine list... that's one of the best in London"

and topped off with a wine list, assembled by award-winning sommelier Matthieu Longuere, that's one of the best in London, with a good selection by the glass and lots of half bottles and – should you require it – all the guidance you'll ever need for menu matching.

5–7 Devonshire Road, Chiswick, W4 2EU

Tel: 020 8747 1836 www.latrompette.co.uk   £53

Open: noon (12.30pm Sun)–2.30pm (3pm Sun), 6.30–10.30pm

Umu

Kyoto Japanese

Be pampered/Clandestine rendevous/Make an impression/When someone else pays

The entrance to another MARC production – The Greenhouse (see page 73) is subtle but it's nothing compared to this slick secretive Japanese beauty. In the corner of a quiet residential mews, its door is a sliding touch sensitive affair that can be opened by a discreet button - if you want to look cool – or – and this is how most enter first time – pawing at it like a confused child. Once inside it's very, very quiet. It's a Japanese restaurant unlike Nobu (see page 101) or Zuma (see page 163) or Roka (see page 121) in that the atmosphere comes with the food and not vice versa. There's a lake of sake, and a sommelier to give you a guided tour

"a very relaxing place, like Switzerland but with sake lakes"

around it. It's really a very relaxing place, like Switzerland but with sake lakes and exquisite Japanese food. Which, I imagine, is what Kyoto is like.

14–16 Bruton Place, Mayfair, W1J 6LX
Tel: 020 7499 8881   www.umurestaurant.com   £112
Open: noon–2.30pm, 6–11pm Mon–Fri; 6–11pm Sat

Viet Grill

Vietnamese

Frugal feasting/Quintessential London

The sequel to Cay Tre on Old Street, the Viet Grill is the most grown-up Vietnamese amongst the cluster that forms the Little Hanoi stretch of Kingsland Road. Sure you've got to love Sông Quê (see page 130) but the place is chaotic fun not reliable restaurant. Not that Viet Grill is necessarily that yet but they've got themselves a

new modern interior, Malcom Gluck recommending wines to go with the food, and they've even got online discount vouchers on the flash new website they share with Cay Tre. They're making the effort and they're going places. Sadly they also seem to have dropped most of the lost in translation style menu descriptions, the only snigger com-

"Saigon torch-roast pork belly and special Vietnamese quail curry"

ing with 'shaking beef'. Reading the rest of the menu only makes you hungry. Saigon torch roast pork belly and the special Vietnamese quail curry – in particular.

58 Kingsland Road, Hackney, E2 8DP
Tel: 020 7739 6686 www.vietnamesekitchen.co.uk   £29
Open: daily, noon–3pm, 5.30–11pm

Map
C

Villandry

French

Breakfast/On-the-hoof

The multi-facteted Villandry – all cream stone floors and tall, whitewashed walls – is a takeaway deli with fine cheese and charcuterie, a posh grocery store with its own line of products, bar and a 100-cover restaurant.

Smack bang in the middle of Great Portland Street, the weekday buzz comes from office workers and BBC media types popping in for lunch and yummy mummies, pushing prams past the expensive produce. If you've got the money they'll even put a hamper together for a picnic in nearby Regent's Park. It's posh picnic food that they excel at, when it comes to grabbing a bite on

"breakfast on everything, from soft-boiled egg and soldiers to smoked Scottish kippers"

the run – or so says restaurant industry head hunter, Guillaume Rochette of Eureka and the Greenhouse's executive chef, Antonin Bonnet. You can also breakfast on everything, from soft-boiled egg and soldiers to smoked Scottish kippers, at the 40-seat bar.

170 Great Portland Street, Marylebone, W1W 5QB
Tel: 020 7631 3131 www.villandry.com   £38
Open: noon–3pm, 6–10.30pm Mon–Sat; 11.30am–4pm Sun

Vinoteca

Abuse the wine list

Smart Smithfield wine bar cum wine shop that doesn't take itself too seriously, despite having an excellent 275-strong global list of wines from small suppliers. Particular attention is given to France, Italy and Spain but

"Interesting long list, fair prices, sound food." – Fay Maschler

there's also a decent New World selection and even room for smaller wine nations such as England. You sit surrounded by shelves of wine and order from a daily changing blackboard menu overseen by chef Carol Craddock (ex of Bibendum see page 32) that might include dishes such as dressed Cornish crab, duck confit or slow-roast pork belly. Glasses of wine, of which there is a rotating selection of 25 available each week, start at £2.95, with the mark-ups on bottles considerably lower than at the average restaurant. Fay Maschler, restaurant critic of *The Evening Standard,* sums it up thus, "Interesting long list, fair prices, sound food."

7 St John St, Clerkenwell, EC1M 4AA
Tel: 020 7253 8786 www.vinoteca.co.uk   £28
Open: noon–11pm. Closed Sundays.

Wahaca

Mexican

Frugal feasting

We're still waiting for quality Mexican food to hit big in London but Wahaca, along with, in a more boho way, Crazy Homies (see page 57), have helped make it seem cool by producing food that's light years away from the piss-poor Tex-Mex, that passed for Mexican food over here not so long ago. Wahaca is a sprawling, affordable, and hence packed, Covent Garden canteen that does 'Mexican market eating'. Fronted by the telegenic Master Chef winner, Thomasina Miers, it has a huge menu

of Mexican staples, mostly designed for shar-

"Wahaca is a sprawling, affordable, and hence packed"

ing, that, from the guacamole up, are freshly made with care. Char-grilled rump steak *tacos*, salmon *ceviche tostadas*, slow-cooked pork *burritos* and Coloradito *mole enchilada* give you a flavour of, otherwise unpronounceable for us Brits, Oaxaca. All meat is British, the chicken and pork free-range, and, local buying sorts that they are, they even use chillies from Devon.

66 Chandos Place, Covent Garden, WC2N 4HG
Tel: 020 7240 1883   www.wahaca.co.uk   £27
Open: daily, noon–11pm (10.30pm Sun)

Wapping Food

Modern Eclectic

Lazy Sunday/Quintessential London/Worth the schlep

Decommissioned hydraulic power station turned exhibition space and restaurant, the Wapping Project opened in 2000. The Australian-run restaurant and bar sits in its modern interior within the old turbine hall, surrounded by corroded machinery, all sea green peeling paint and cracked rusty gauges. The customers are a motley mix of City boys, curious tourists and scattering of arty locals. The menu veers all over the place, in a typically antipodean fashion, from watermelon and feta salad, to chorizo, black pudding and squid, and balsamic ice cream for dessert. On Sunday's the lunch is very popular; fans include Marina

"Great food, a magnificent place and does cracking bloody Marys." – Marina O'Loughlin

O'Loughlin, *Metro*'s restaurant critic, who goes because it's "great food, a magnificent place and does cracking bloody Marys". While food writer Caroline Stacey chooses it for a one-off London experience because it's a "jaw dropping building – like a mini Tate Modern".

Wapping Hydraulic Power Station, Wapping Wall, E1
Tel: 020 7680 2080   www.thewappingproject.com   £38
Open: noon–3.30pm, 6.30–11pm Mon–Fri; 10am–4pm,
7–11pm Sat; 10am–4pm Sun

Wild Honey
Modern British

Abuse the wine list/Be pampered/Dine solo/Wish they'd thought of it

No change to the winning formula that brought lavish critical praise, bucket loads of awards and an oversubscribed dining room for this, the follow up to Arbutus (see page 20) from the seemingly effortlessly successful chef and front-of-house partnership of Anthony Demetre and Will Smith. Sure the former Drones Club's Mayfair premises (Wild Honey being a cryptic reference to the building's past) are oak-panelled, high-ceilinged and la-di-da grand compared with Arbutus' more modest and modern Soho home. But the

"fine French technique from the kitchen in dishes that make the most out of the seasons"

price-sensitive approach (set three-course lunch for £16.95 or £18.95 for three course pre theatre), friendly service, plat du jour, fine French technique from the kitchen in dishes that make the most out of the seasons, a wine list that offers every selection in 250ml carafes and the opportunity to eat at the bar if you're on your tod, all remains intact.

12 St George Street, Mayfair, W1S 2FB
Tel: 020 7758 9160   www.wildhoneyrestaurant.co.uk   £44
Open: noon–2.30pm (3pm Sun), 6–10.30pm (9.30pm Sun)

The Wolseley

Breakfast/Dine solo/Make an impression/ People watch/Quintessential London/Wish they'd thought of it

An overwhelmingly popular breakfast venue, many never

"*it's also about the setting, a sumptuous film set of a room*"

go to The Wolseley for lunch and dinner, although it is typically full for both. The recently published recipe book *Breakfast at The Wolseley*, isn't going to help them shake off the image of being a morning place. But they're not worried – there's money to be made in bacon and eggs. There's much comfort to a huge morning menu that offers crumpets, Cumberland sausage sandwiches, crispy bacon rolls, eggs Benedict, fried haggis with duck eggs, omelette Arnold Bennett – to name but a fraction of what's on offer. But it's also about the setting, a sumptuous film set of a room on Piccadilly, that was a once car show room for the marque it's now named after, modelled into a sweeping European grand café. The Wolseley is currently *the* place to see and be seen, and while dining is of the essence sometimes you just can't help peering curiously at your neighbours.

160 Piccadilly, Mayfair, W1J 9EB
Tel: 020 7499 6996 www.thewolseley.com   £45
Open: daily, 7am (8am Sat/Sun)–midnight (11pm Sun)

Wonder Bar   Modern wine bar

Abuse the wine list

You've got to love Westminster Trading Standards who, apparently with nothing better to do back in the summer of 2007, decided to piss on the parade that was the opening of Selfridge's new wine bar and shop. They didn't like their 'Enomatic Wine System' (see The East Room, page 63) or so-called wine jukebox, which dispensed thimblefuls of some of the world's most expensive wines – a 1996 Petrus for £32 a sip, for instance. Sadly the law states, as the jobworths noted, that wine must be sold in 175ml or 250ml measures and so their

machine has been recalibrated to serve only full glasses. If you

"some of the world's most expensive wines – a 1996 Petrus for £32 a sip"

don't fancy the wine jukebox, full bottles are available to drink in the bar at the wine shop at retail price plus £10 corkage, and there are plates of cheese, charcuterie and smoked fish available to graze on.

Selfridges, 400 Oxford Street, Marylebone, W1A 1AB
Tel: 0800 123 400 www.selfridges.com   £32
Open: 9.30am (11am Sun)–8pm (9pm Thurs/Sat, 6pm Sun)

Wright Brothers Oyster & Porter house

Clandestine rendezvous/Quintessential London

Oyster suppliers to some of London's finest restaurants, the Wright Brothers decided to open a little place of their own in 2005. On the edge of Borough Market, from where they also run their wholesale business, Wright Brothers is essentially a vibrant bar, just one that has the largest selection of oysters on sale you're ever likely to

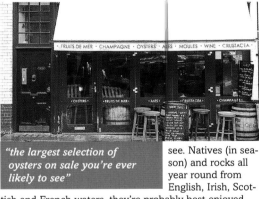

"the largest selection of oysters on sale you're ever likely to see"

see. Natives (in season) and rocks all year round from English, Irish, Scottish and French waters, they're probably best enjoyed sitting at the bar with a glass of stout, porter or champagne. Moving beyond oysters – although before doing it's worth mentioning that their oyster rarebit comes highly recommended – the menu tends to keep it simple and sticks mostly to seafood with dressed crab, smoked salmon and fish pie. The one meaty exception being the beef, Guinness and – you guessed it – oyster pie.

11 Stoney Street, Southwark, SE1 9AD
Tel: 020 7403 9554   www.wrightbros.eu.com   £41
Open: noon–10.30pm. Closed Sundays.

Map C

Yauatcha

Modern Cantonese

Dine solo/On-the-hoof/People watch/Wish they'd thought of it

Alan Yau's take on the Taipei teahouse took the Cantonese custom of dim sum from an afternoon to an all-day event. But unlike the chains it's inspired since it opened in 2004, Yauatcha produces arguably the best dim sum in town. Spread over the ground floor and basement of a modish Richard Rodgers office block on the corner of Berwick Street Market, the downstairs dining room is a stunner, all over-sized fish tank bar and sparkly lights in the ceiling. The more minimalistic and relaxed upstairs lounge, where the full menu is also available, serves and sells high-end Franco-Asian patisserie, which

"Yauatcha produces arguably the best dim sum in town"

you can wash down with a world-class tea list. The waiters wear *Crouching Tiger*-inspired uniforms (Yau used the same designer) and the dim sum itself, from the venison puffs to the steamed scallop and kumquat dumpling, is exceptional.

15 Broadwick Street, Soho, W1F 0DL
Tel: 0870 780 8265 www.yauatcha.com   £38
Open: daily, 11am–11.45pm (10.30pm Sun)

Zuma

E

**Dine solo/Make an impression/People watch/
When someone else pays/Wish they'd thought
of it**

A modern Japanese restaurant conceived by a London-
based German chef and which now has branches in
Hong Kong, Istanbul and Dubai. Opened in 2002, Reiner
Becker's Knightsbridge Japanese was immediately an

ambitious proposi-
tion, its interior a
striking mixture of
glass, stone and
wood and the
menu made it
clear that it was
taking on Nobu.
An overnight des-
tination for the
very rich and the
very thin, the bar
and lounge be-
came an instant
scene. Eating
alone at the sushi
counter is perhaps
the best place to
watch it all unfold.
The menu is divid-

*"an overnight destination for the
very rich and the very thin"*

ed into small dishes and salads, sushi and *sashimi*, robata
grill bits and pieces, and what are labelled 'Zuma' dishes
that comprise east meets west combinations such as
seared miso marinated foie gras with *umeboshi* compote.
It's all as expensive as it sounds. Make someone else pay
if you can.

5 Raphael Street, Knightsbridge, SW7 1DL
Tel: 020 7584 1010 www.zumarestaurant.com   £62
Open: daily, noon (12.30pm Sun)—2.15pm (2.45pm Fri,
3.15pm Sat/Sun), 6–11pm (10pm Sun)

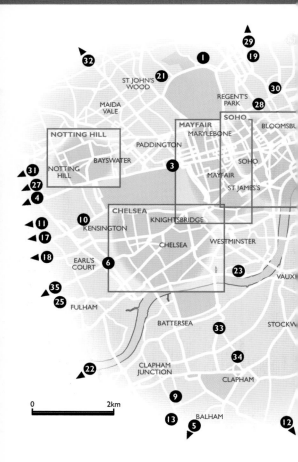

ST JOHN'S WOOD

MAIDA VALE

NOTTING HILL

BAYSWATER

NOTTING HILL

PADDINGTON

REGENT'S PARK

MAYFAIR

MARYLEBONE

SOHO

BLOOMSBU

SOHO

MAYFAIR

ST JAMES'S

CHELSEA

KENSINGTON

KNIGHTSBRIDGE

CHELSEA

WESTMINSTER

EARL'S COURT

VAUXI

FULHAM

BATTERSEA

STOCKW

CLAPHAM JUNCTION

CLAPHAM

BALHAM

0   2km

SHOREDITCH

WHITECHAPEL

BERMONDSEY

ROTHERHITHE

WALWORTH

CAMBERWELL

12. Le Cassoulet
13. Chez Bruce
14. Faulkner's
15. Food Lab
16. The Garrison
17. Indian Zing
18. Mango & Silk
19. Market
20. Numara Bos Cirrik
21. Oslo Court
22. Petersham Nurseries
23. Pomegranates
24. Rasa
25. The River Café
26. RSJ
27. Sagar
28. Snazz Sichuan
29. St. John's Tavern
30. St Pancras
    Champagne Bar
31. Sushi Hiro
32. Sushi Say
33. Tom Illic
34. Trinity
35. La Trompette
36. Wapping Food

1. L'Absinthe
2. Anchor & Hope
3. Angelus
4. Anglesea Arms
5. Apollo Banana Leaf
6. Bar Asia
7. Best Turkish Kebab
8. Bistrotheque
9. Boiled Egg & Soldiers
10. Byron
11. The Carpenter's Arms

0   250m   500m

⊖ Underground
  Station

1. The Albemarle
2. Atari-Ya
3. Beirut Express
4. Benares
5. Bentley's
6. Brasserie St. Jacques
7. Le Caprice
8. Cecconi's
9. China Tang (Dorchester)
10. Cipriani

11. Defune
12. Dinings
13. Galvin Bistrot de Luxe
14. Galvin at Windows
15. La Gavroche
16. The Greenhouse
17. Green's St James
18. Hibiscus
19. Japan Centre (Toku)
20. Locanda Locatelli
21. Maroush I
22. Maze
23. Momo
24. Nobu (Park Lane)
25. La Petite Maison
26. El Pirata
27. Ranoush
28. Sake no Hana
29. Scott's
30. Sketch
31. The Square
32. Tamarind
33. Theo Randall
34. Trader Vic's
35. Umu
36. Wild Honey
37. The Wolseley
38. Wonder Bar

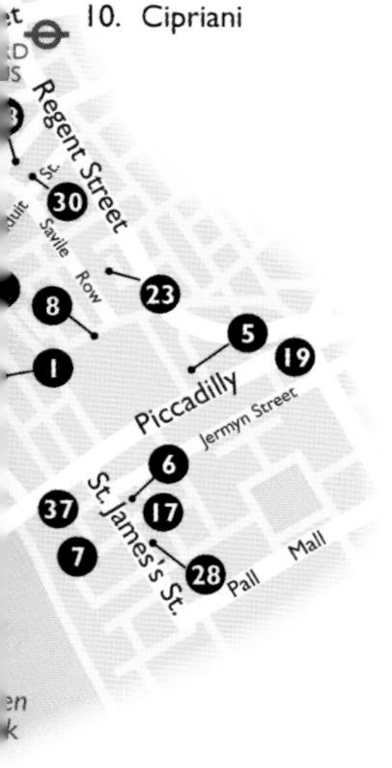

Regent Street

Savile Row

30

8   23

1

5   19

Piccadilly

Jermyn Street

6

37   17

7   28

St. James's St.

Pall Mall

GOODGE
STREET

Russ
Sq. G

Place
Malet

Torrington
Gower Street

Street

Cleveland
Maple Street

Howland
Street

Tottenham Court Road

Bedford
Square

Bloomsbury

31

Goodge Street

25 **22**

Mortimer   Street

Berners

Newman Street

Street

Street

Regent Street

Gt. Portland St.

Eastcastle Street

Street

15

TOTTENHAM
COUT ROAD

OXFORD
CIRCUS

Oxford   Street

19

Charing   Cross   Road

Soho
Square

23

Gt. Marlborough St.

5

7

2

Frith Street

17 **8**

Monmouth Street

Earlham

6

24

St.

3

12 **9**

Broadwick St.

33

Wardour

Old   Compton

St.

4

30

1

26

Regent   Street

13

Avenue

10

20 **21**

LEICESTER
SQUARE

16

28

Shaftesbury

Street

Brewer

11

Whitcomb   Street

Leicester
Square

PICCADILLY
CIRCUS

27

Haymarket

Trafalgar
Square

CHARING N

0   250m   500m

⊖ Underground
Station

Pall   Mall

CHARING
CROSS

Map C

1. Andrew Edmunds
2. Arbutus
3. L'Atelier de Joël Robuchon
4. Bar Shu
5. Barrafina
6. Bodean's
7. Busaba Eathai
8. Café Boheme
9. Cha Cha Moon
10. Chinese Experience
11. Chinese Restaurant 1997
12. Dehesa
13. Donzoko
14. Great Queen Street
15. Hakkasan
16. J Sheekey
17. Jen Café
18. Joe Allen
19. Mr Jerk
20. Mr Kong
21. New Diamond
22. Pied A Terre
23. Pizza Malletti
24. Quo Vadis
25. Roka
26. Shampers
27. St. Alban
28. Taro
29. The Terrace
30. Tokyo Diner
31. Villandry
32. Wahaca
33. Yauatcha

0   200m

Underground
Station

ROYAL OAK

Westbourne Park Villas

Westbourne Park Road

Porchester Road

Sunderland T.

Newton Rd.

Westbourne Grove

Queensway

Redan Pl.

Inverness T.

Garway Road

Hereford Road

Porchester Gdns.

BAYSWATER

Moscow Road

Bark Pl.

Palace Court

Ossington St.

Hill Gate

1. Assaggi
2. Le Café Anglais
3. Costas Fish Restaurant
4. The Cow
5. Crazy Homies
6. The Electric Brasserie
7. Hereford Road
8. Hung Tao
9. Kiasu
10 Lucky 7
11 Royal China
12 Tom's Deli

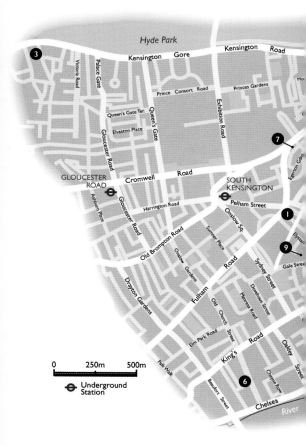

Hyde Park

Kensington Gore

Kensington Road

3

Victoria Road

Palace Gate

Prince Consort Road

Princes Gardens

Mo

Queen's Gate Ter.

Queen's Gate

Exhibition Road

Elvaston Place

Gloucester Road

7

Eggerton Garus

GLOUCESTER ROAD

Cromwell   Road

SOUTH KENSINGTON

Ashburn Place

Gloucester Road

Harrington Road

Pelham Street

Onslow Sq.

1

Elysta

9

Gale Street

Old Brompton Road

Sumner Place

Onslow Gardens

Road

Sydney Street

Drayton Gardens

Fulham

Old Church Street

Manresa Road

Dovehouse Street

Oakley

Road

Elm Park Road

Street

King's

Road

Cheyne Row

Park Walk

6

Beaufort Street

Chelsea

River

0   250m   500m

⊖ Underground Station

172

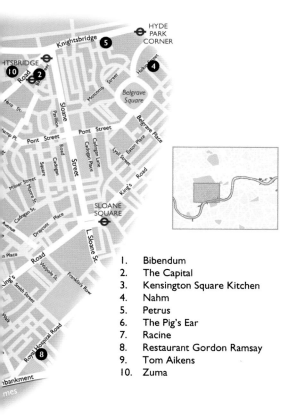

1. Bibendum
2. The Capital
3. Kensington Square Kitchen
4. Nahm
5. Petrus
6. The Pig's Ear
7. Racine
8. Restaurant Gordon Ramsay
9. Tom Aikens
10. Zuma

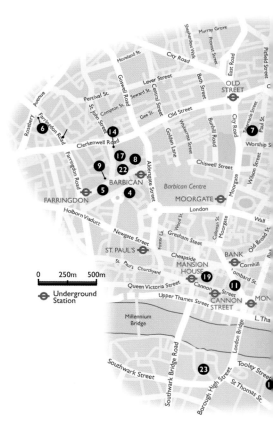

1. L'Anima
2. Beigel Bake
3. Blueprint Café
4. Club Gascon
5. Comptoir Gascon
6. The Eagle
7. The East Room
8. The Fox & Anchor
9. Hix Oyster
   & Chop House
10. Lahore Kebab House
11. London Capital Club
12. Magdalen
13. E Pellicci
14. Pho
15. Rochelle Canteen
16. Song Que
17. St John
18. St John Bread & Wine
19. Sweetings
20. Tayyabs
21. Viet Grill
22. Vinoteca
23. Wright Bros